THE BEAST

WHITE SUPREMACY

James Omolo

Edition published by

Cosmodernity Consultants

Copyright © 2020 by James Omolo

An imprint of Cosmodernity Consultants LLC

Cover credit: Samir Saadi

Editing: Dominika Pasterska

First printing: 2020

ISBN-978-83-947118-2-5

Universal Declaration of Human Rights

Everyone is entitled to all the rights and freedoms set forth in this Declaration, without distinction of any kind, such as race, colour, sex, language, religion, political or other opinion, national or social origin, property, birth or other status.

INTRODUCTION

———

The Beast: *White Supremacy* is a book about variegated controversial topics in race relations. It delves into the world of White supremacy, capturing its all-encompassing centrality, assumed superiority and the practices based on this assumption.

It builds on the premise of race relations with the aim of confronting some of the prevalent elements of white supremacy so as to prompt white people to take action against the harm being inflicted upon Black people.

Moreover, this book hopes to provide a better understanding of white supremacy and to take the concept into even deeper conversation by offering a historical and cultural context, and how these contexts influence contemporary society.

In the grand scheme, white supremacy in Europe is a prominent ideological phenomenon with social and political implications, whereby right-wing governments instrumentalise institutions to further their ideologies for political gain. This political structure has considerable ramifications for the life chances of Black people.

Is Europe reliving its dark Holocaust history? The events which have unfolded since the refugee crisis of 2015, have been a strong reminder that the slogan *'Never Again'* , intended to isolate the horrors of the past, is being compromised. Recent events have shown the many desperate situations which have arisen, from violent attacks on immigrants of African origin to a lack of acknowledgment and denial of racism. The reasons for these developments are also multiple, from official ideologies such as nationalism to prejudice towards minorities.

What makes this book exceptional is how it attempts to connect historical perspectives with their implications for contemporary race relations; problems premised upon white supremacy, outlining various parentheses to validate the narratives.

As a Black man, race has always been an integral part of my life. I have been the object of curiosity and unwarranted treatment by white supremacists. My blackness is served up with the menu of my sartorial style, visits to revellers joints, the type of music I listen to, the local places I hangout in. The riches that come with belonging to a variant race never satisfy my thirst for humanity even though these experiences have been important. My unsatiated thirst for social justice, equality and equity has been my passion despite the constant haranguing by some people in my addressing these issues. What I write or say may often be discomforting for many White people, but I vow always to stick my neck out.

This personal conviction has motivated my activism for seeking ways in which to create awareness and make a positive contribution to the plight of people of African Descent in Poland and Europe in general.

My experience of racism can be traced back many years to when I was a student in India. At the time I had a warped sense of my own identity and self-worth due to the everyday prejudices which habitually subject Black people to pejorative comments. The problem was that few people wanted to acknowledge the existence of racism, fewer still talked about it and even the African community was tacit in its acceptance. Issues of race and racism often took a back seat. Although of a different trajectory, the racism in those times did not reach the magnitude I now experience living in Europe and particularly in Poland where I have lived for more than a decade. It has been during my years in Poland that I have experienced the kind of complex and arcane discrimination faced by the Black community in Europe. For this reason, I focus on this dominant factor by providing solid moral and political arguments to counter the abhorrent practices that a vast number of the Black community are forced to experience as a result of white supremacy.

Living in Europe, it dawned upon me that I have been made to feel like a hidden lumbering monster. The purveyors of white supremacy continue to spread their messages of fear and hatred. They repudiate us with vile, hateful and racist rhetoric and actions. It is the derogatory comments about my physical attributes, about being an African, about my perceived affiliation to primates that often invite monkey chants on the street, my looks becoming a barometer for my performance. It feels surreal that I have to be an ambassador for the entire African continent.

My blackness does not protect me from security guards who follow me in stores as I shop, suspecting me of stealing merchandise. I always wear the badge of 'suspect citizen'. The notion that Black people are genetically predisposed to thievery and being treated like criminals feels like a living hell.,

My perceived race does not shield me from being stopped by the police or scrutinized at the airport under the pretense of random checks nor does it protect me from working many years without a promotion or sometimes being paid less than my white colleagues with fewer qualifications.

As I consider my commute t to work, school or for any other reason, my mind becomes fraught with anxiety, frustration and anger at the thought of being targeted.

As a Black man, I have to bear the burden of having to be twice as good to get half as far, and my heart sinks at the thought that if status quo remains unchallenged, I will continue to carry this burden for the rest of my life..

The constant, echoing voices of 'go back to Africa' become an incessant reminder that I do not belong here, that I will forever be a stranger in the country I have embraced as my second home.

And when my two children were born, I felt the nagging certainty of what they are going to face in a prejudiced mono-racial society, bearing in mind that they are already categorized as Black even though they are mixed-race. They are just as white as they are Black. Racial misrecognition is particularly salient for individuals with Black and White heritage. I am holding my own sorrow for my own little children in which their brown skin does not matter to anyone with any power; their pain, falling on deaf ears.

As a Black man and an author, I am necessarily absorbed by writing books of which I am a subject as well as writing about my environment; books that project the personal lives of diverse characters. Race has been one of the most defining aspects of my life and it is something I have been profoundly vocal about whether in Poland or elsewhere. I continue to talk about it unequivocally, even though I experience many obstacles. However, before I became engaged in activism, I, like many other People of African Descent (PAD), was just trying to eke out a living and minding my own business. There is work, kids, activities at home and friends, and sometimes the cost of balancing these responsibilities while focusing on activism could be costly. However, I am not ready to sell my conscience. My enduring desire to effect a positive contribution upon the existing status quo remains undiminished and is the driving force throughout my engagements.

Micro aggressions are the most common manifestations of racism and carry considerable psychological ramifications and pain, the term microsgressions is debatable considering its consequences. These occur very commonly in social places especially on the street; monkey chants, insults, nigger calling and go back to your country rhetoric are just a few of the dimensions of the microaggressions.

It is indeed a rough and bumpy road being a Black person in the West. One day I said to myself that, the moment I feel a relief from the manifestations of racism will be the moment I make a hell of a noise in jubilation. This moment has yet to arrive, so I am putting more effort into writing and addressing these issues in order to create awareness around the world. It also helps to relieve me of some of the things that weigh me down. My activisms also something therapeutic; -a problem shared is a problem half-solved, I suppose.

White supremacy is a prominent ideological phenomenon in Europe with social and political ramifications, whereby right-wing governments instrumentalize institutions to further their ideologies for political gain.

Whilst in Italy in 2018, Mussolini loyalists went on a shooting rampage in the streets of Macerata. A gunman, identified as a former local candidate for Italy's Far-Right Northern league, went on a drive-by shooting spree that left six African migrants wounded.[1]

> ""We shouldn't forget that the people who are coming here grew up in a different religion and represent a completely different culture. Most are not Christian, but Muslim,"......"Or is it not worrying that Europe's Christian culture is already barely able to maintain its own set of Christian values?"...**Hungarian Prime Minister Viktor Orbán**

In Hungary, Viktor Orban is continuing to gain popularity with his anti-immigration campaigns, expelling billionaire

George Soros, founder of the Open Society Foundation, a democracy watchdog organization. Orban also infringes the constitutional court and fires up Far-right groups with ammunition.

> *Migrants have brought diseases like cholera and dysentery to Europe, as well as "all sorts of parasites and protozoa, which ... while not dangerous in the organisms of these people, could be dangerous here."...Jarosław Kaczyński, former Polish Prime Minister and leader of the Law and Justice party[2].*

Poland and Hungary have enjoyed cordial relations since as early as the Middle Ages, entrenched as they were in shared rulers, cultures and faith. In fact, every year on March 23, both countries mark their fraternal relationship. However, this 'bromance' between the current administrations is questionable. Their fight in the political realm on a macro-scale seems to be well coordinated with considerable similarities in their actions, from their hard stance on taking in refugees to the crackdown on civil society to constitutional courts and media freedoms.

On January 20 2020, the European Parliament even released a press-briefing warning that the rule of law in Poland and Hungary had worsened and that the two countries were not aligned with the EU's founding values[3]. Their actions are performative rather than transformative.

In France, Marine Le Pen, the daughter of a convicted Holocaust denier and the President of the National Rally political party since 2011, took second place in the last presidential election. She is outspoken on immigration, openly anti-Semitic and uses nationalistic rhetoric. She is also open to making France a homogeneous white society. In the 2017 presidential election she took a hard line when she advocated for an immediate suspension of all legal immigration. Unfortunately, many of her ideas have become profoundly mainstream[4].

> *"Germany probably thinks its population is moribund and it is probably seeking to lower wages and continue to recruit slaves through mass immigration,"....*
>
> **Marine Le Pen, leader of the National Front[5]**

In Germany, (once the bedrock of Nazism) the city of Berlin bears witness to the Holocaust. In an 800 square meter information centre located on a stretch of the former death strip (where the Wall once stood near the Brandenburg Gate), is Berlin's Holocaust Memorial. The memorial has the personal documentation of individuals and families murdered in the genocide. And yet today the anti-Muslim Far-right is rapidly increasing in Germany, with most observers also of the opinion that the country is grappling with the spectre of rising Anti-Semitism. Thirty years after the fall of the Berlin wall, Germany is still divided, with the Eastern part being more intolerant to immigrants than the Western part of the country..

"Let's not forget, the Syrian who comes to us has still his Syria,". "The Afghan who comes to us has still his Afghanistan [...] but if we lose our Germany, then we have no more homes!" **BjörnHöcke, head of the Alternative for Germany (AFD)**[6]

Is Europe reliving its dark history? The events which have unfolded since the refugee crisis of 2015 have been a palpable reminder that the slogan *'Never Again '*is being compromised. Particularly with the rise of neo-Nazism, fascism and government supported Anti-Semitism we see that Europe has not changed for the better. And that indeed, Europe is (re)writing its own history.

Recent events in Europe have shown many desperate situations, from violent attacks on immigrants to a lack of acknowledgement and denial of racism. The reasons are varied, from ideologies such as nationalism to prejudice towards minorities. In fact, there appears to be considerable unity among nationalists and far right groups or parties when it comes to anti-immigrant issues.

CHAPTER ONE

The Racist Hybrid

NO SOUL WITH A MODICUM of consciousness would refute that racism, a system that promotes domination and subjugation, has been a human problem for centuries and that it has increased exponentially in recent times.

In a remote part of Northern Poland, a young man of Polish-African heritage was walking along a beach with his White Polish friends when suddenly an old man approached him and asked, "Who is the monkey? The old man pressed the button of racism and prejudice that left the young man in complete shock. It was surreal. For the young man, the ramifications of this incident were that of a vile emotional abuse. He was stunned by the prevalence of racism in modern Poland, a country the young man calls home.

The prevalence of prejudice and racism often leads to far more egregious events. If we were to recall history; six million Jews were murdered because it was believed they were lesser human beings; approximately a million people massacred in Rwanda over a three-month period because a group of people considered them subhuman and did not believe they deserved to live. Millions of African people were bought and sold as slaves, kidnapped, raped and tortured during the Transatlantic and Tran-Saharan slave trade in order to develop the wealth of Europe and America. This happened because it was believed that these people were of an inferior race. The actions of invaders were justified through a combination of science, physiological classification and cultural evaluation designed to categorise humanity along racial lines.

One chilly morning, back in my university days when I was feeling tired after a long night of clubbing, my cousin, a friend and I were just dreaming of getting back to our hostel to get some sleep. This was one of those moments when the inevitable happens and when the gods are not on your side. Dragging our heavy feet halfway to the bus stop, a group of middle-aged individuals confronted us. They spat on me and my cousin, and shouted, "White power. Go back to Africa,"- words so excruciatingly painful that they reduce one to tears. This pack of men was angry, seething with rage. We were startled and trembling with anger and frustration as well. I could also feel the venom of their hate in their words. The insults were intended to condemn and hurt us, to make us feel subhuman and to show us we were being treated as social pariahs.

This was just the beginning of years of physical attacks, insults, monkey chants and nigger-calling which just went on and on. Thirteen years later, I still experience these kinds of attacks and affronts. My long stay in Poland has not inoculated me against these social realities. And this is a feeling that is shared by a vast number of People of African Descent in Poland and the rest of Europe who are disdained as an inferior race.

Discourse on racism in Poland and other parts of Europe has been overlooked for many years simply because it was perceived that racism was subtle, that slowly it will fade and that it does not need to be addressed because Poles and other

Europeans are not racist. How could Poles be racist when they have been and are still victims of subjugation by their Western European counterparts, some would say.

For many years, racism has escalated from being subtle to more egregious and by extension, insidious. Right-wing ideology is certainly more prevalent now than it was 14 years ago when I first arrived in Europe. Certainly there are more anti-immigrant groups now than there were thirteen years ago. What has gone wrong? My response is that the current political situation has provided a breeding ground for the Far-right and nationalistic ideologies to mushroom. I liken it to a bottle of Coca Cola; when shaken, it will explode.

Racism has existed in a variety of forms and trajectories over the course of Europe's history. In recent times there have been incidences of Anti-Semitism, Islamophobia, physical attacks on people of African Descent. The list is long. I have heard many Africans equating racism to ignorance and a lack of contact. In my view, racism is about power dynamics. The idea that racism is the result of locals having had little contact with foreigners and stems rather from suspicion and ignorance than hatred seems to me to be baseless. We know that prejudice is not rational. People perceive others through their own lenses. If it is about contact, then metropolitan cities like London, New York, Sydney etc would be racism-free.

The popular use of the word racism is relatively recent. The term was coined in the 1930s, primarily as a response to the Nazi project of making Germany *judenrein,* or 'clean of Jews'[7]. The Nazis believed that the Jews were a different race and were a threat to the Aryan race to which real Germans belonged. The notion of racism is meticulously interlinked to the concept of race. The term racism has also emerged from social forces and political conflicts[8].

The following definition of racism from the eminent British biologist Steven Rose, outlines the significant doctrines of race from the 11th Century onwards;

By race is meant any claim of the natural superiority of one identifiable human population, group or race over another. By "scientific racism" is meant the attempt to use the language and some of the techniques of science in support of theories or contentions that particular groups or populations are innately inferior to others in terms of intelligence, or civilization or other socially-defined attitudes[9].

In his 1903 book, *The Souls of Black Folk,* W.E.B. Dubois argued that, white racism has generated a type of double consciousness: the sense of always looking at one self through the eyes of others. It incorporates the notion that an individual's consciousness and one's world are always spoken for, narrativized before the fact and appropriated by the surrounding white society[10]. He coined this term at the end of the American Revolution, when African Americans were 'officially' freed from slavery by Abraham Lincoln. Due to the tendencies of White supremacy, Black people started looking at themselves through the eyes of white people and convinced themselves of their inferiority. Later however, they developed self-consciousness, developing skills in music, poetry, literature and plays in an effort to express their everyday experiences and challenges at the hands of white people and white governance . According to Dubois, it was this building of alliances and movements that produced the Harlem Renaissance.

European institutions are still predominantly white. In fact, of the 2014-2019 Parliament, only 17 of 751 members of the European Parliament,(around 2 %) were People of African Descent. In 2019, Claude Moraes, a British Member of the European Parliament, reiterated the overwhelming whiteness of this institution and that no person of African descent had ever been appointed a Commissioner, revealing the often blatantly ignored structural discrimination facing minorities across Europe[11].

It is also disconcerting that those who are mandated to enact laws and policies are the very people who are abusing their office and subjugating persons of colour by virtue of being white. A good example of this is Cecile Kyenge, (whom I have personally met).Ms Kyenge is an iron lady and the first Black Member of the Italian Parliament. In 2018, in an interview with The Guardian newspaper, she gave an account of her experiences;

> *Since my election to the Italian Chamber of Deputies in 2013, I have constantly faced racist abuse. When I became Italy's Minister of Integration, as the country's first Black minister, it got worse. A fellow Italian MEP, Mario Borghezio, called my appointment 'a*

shitty choice' by a 'bongo bongo' government, adding that I had the 'face of a housewife'[12].

In France, racism is a latent problem for Black lawmakers. France's colonial heritage still predominates in both institutional and societal structures. Ms Christiane Taubira, the French justice minister who was born in French Guiana once gave an account of how she had been taunted by children waving banana skins and compared to a monkey by a National Front mayoral candidate[13]. This kind of racism has dire consequences for social cohesion, not to mention the dampening of spirits of many People of African Descent and their disincentivisation from active engagement in politics.

Magid Magid knows very well how it feels to be discriminated at the top institution in the continent. Magid, a 30-year old, newly elected member of the European Parliament for the Green Party from Yorkshire and Humber had his activism put to the test on the very day he arrived for the inauguration of the new legislatures. With his signature baseball cap, and a T shirt, reading 'F**k fascism', it was reported that he was asked to leave the European Parliament building by an official. He said that the official asked if he was lost and then suggested he leave. Magid later stated that he did not leave and underlined that this kind of reaction reflected people's assumptions about what a 'typical' politician is meant to look like. [14]. After the incident, he took to Twitter to express his dismay;

I know I'm visibly (Sic) different. I don't have the privilege to hide my identity. I'm BLACK and my name is Magid. I do not intend to try to fit in. Get used to it.[15]

Famous Black people and politicians are not insulated from hate speech either. Racially motivated verbal attacks are used as a form of incitement and racial hatred projects are what Black people holding public office experience because of the colour of their skin. There have been derogatory and racist remarks made by well-known white people including some celebrities and politicians. These are people with a platform and influence and making such racist comments just perpetuates racial abuse and hate speech.

Across Europe, the word 'nigger' remains very common in the public domain, from the societal to institutional level. Every country has its own version of the N-word, whilst maintaining that it is not equivalent to the English dictionary definition and not an offensive term in their own language.

The most absurd thing is that it is White people who say their version of the N- word is not offensive, when People of African Descent find the word racially derogatory and highly offensive. Words bear no meaning without a context. The way the N-word is used in the public domain clearly demonstrates its motive to demean and subjugate Black people. Here are some of the ways the N-word has been perennially used by influential people;

The Bavarian Interior Minister in Germany called singer Roberto Blanco a "wonderful negro" on 'Hart Aber Fair', a popular political talk show during a debate on Europe's refugee crisis on one of Germany's most watched public TV stations[16].

The TV host AlbenaVuleva was fined 500 BGN (250 Euros) for stating on TV that Bulgaria is a "White Christian country and is not a nigger country"[17].

In 2014, Swedish elected officials for the liberal party (Moderaterna) decided to bake and sell Swedish oatmeal balls calling them "negerboll"[18].

In the UK, Jeremy Clarkson from the popular show Top Gear used the word "nigger" on the show when reciting the children's nursery rhyme 'Eey, eeny, miny, moe' before apparently mumbling 'catch a nigger by his toe' as he chose between two cars[19].

Even though he later denied using the N-word, as they always do, he was forced later to apologise after growing calls for his resignation.

It soon becomes obvious that the political representation of People of African Descent in Europe is abysmal. Systematic and societal prejudice against Black people makes it hard to enter into politics and when one manages, usually with the help of trusted and friendly white and Black constituents, they become the immediate targets for nationalists. Some Black politicians have been ostracised, racially abused and targeted because of the colour of their skin. This reflects the existential challenges that racism poses even at the highest levels of political structures.

Sport has always been a driving force in promoting the virtues of societies with a strong influence cutting across demographics. It is also invaluable in promoting people to people diplomacy and thus, instrumental for the integration process. However, the stark contradiction is that in Europe, sport has been used as a means to subjugate Black people and other minorities. It has also been rendered a platform where racists can openly exhibit their white supremacy tendencies.

Every football club in Europe has its vile abuse with a continuum of racist slogans supporters hurling racial slurs at Black players. This is not something new to most African football fans. These insults, gestures and chants have been sweeping across European football clubs, a phenomenon that has prompted anti-racist organizations such as 'Football Against Racism in Europe' (FARE NET), to take a strong advocacy stance at European stadiums.

Moussa Marega, a Malian International playing for Portuguese side FC Porto, walked off the pitch on 16 February 2020 after he was racially abused by opposition fans in a match against Vitoria de Guimaraes.

In the Netherlands, a first and second division team did not play the first minute of the matches on the weekend of 23 November 2019 as a protest against racism ensued; a week earlier a match had been suspended for half an hour after a Den Bosch supporter racially abused Excelsior forward Ahmad Mendes Moreira. There was also controversy in Spain on 25 January 2019 when Athletic Bilbao player Inaki Williams was subjected to monkey chants by a section of the home crowd in a game at Espanyol[20].

In February 2020, the BBC released a three-part 'Shame in the Football Game' series, highlighting the prevalence of racism in English football all the way from the premier league to the lower leagues as well as in women's football. The players had different stories with common racist overtones. Several players shared their personal experiences;

> 'They were calling me black monkey, doing monkey signs'-**Inih Effiong, Dover Athletic striker.**

> 'Why is the black lad playing goal? Look at you, you monkey'-**Nathan Ashmore, Boreham Wood FC.**

> 'Smell like curry'-Imrul Gazi, Sporting Bengal... **The manager of a lower league team to an Asian football club based in the UK[21].**

Former Tottenham defender Renee Hecor was racially abused by Sheffield United's Sophie Jones during a championship match in January 2019. After tweeting about the incident, He received a number of racist responses including pictures of monkeys. It is estimated that in the last season (2019), there was a 66% rise in hate crimes reported at professional football games in England and Wales[22].

With such a dubious past and the obvious challenges that people of African Descent face, the community has engaged in various approaches in order to at least address racism and prejudice. Whether through advocacy or awareness-raising campaigns, the community is committed to finding ways to survive this pandemic. A good example is an initiative in Germany, where the hashtag *Me Too* was adapted for a different purpose. They instead used the T-W-0 in English as a hashtag which minorities can use to share their stories of racist abuse. Most of their tweets are accounts of the pervasive nature of discrimination that begins in childhood and progresses though to adulthood.[23]

In order to understand racism, we should differentiate it from prejudice and discrimination. Just like bias, prejudice is composed of feelings, thoughts, including stereotypes, attitudes, and generalizations that are often rooted in little or no experience and are then projected onto everyone from that group. Prejudice can be benign and it may not lead to negative consequences. On the other hand, discrimination implies that one acts on a racist thought. When an employer thinks that Black employees are not trustworthy and avoid appointing Black people to positions where money is involved, this is racism. It is a belief that one race is more trustworthy than another and at the same time it is discrimination as the employer not only believes this to be true, but also acts upon it.

Due to the fact that we all have biases, we are prejudiced to some degree. We all make assumptions based on people's appearances, their hobbies, their educational background, the kind of clothes they wear and their weight, among other things. Our prejudices tend to be shared because we swim in the same cultural water and absorb the same messages. We all have prejudices that we cannot circumvent. If I am cognizant of the presence of a social group, I will endeavour to obtain information from that group and this information will facilitate my understanding of the group from my cultural perspective. People may realize we have more in common than differences once we start to get to know each other better. It should be stressed that those who claim not to be prejudiced are exhibiting a deep-seated deficiency in self-awareness.

Europeans replaced slavery with the pernicious enterprise of 'racism'. The pinnacle of the history of racism occurred in the twentieth century with the emergence of blatantly racist regimes; the ubiquity of segregation laws and restrictions on black voting rights reduced African Americans to lower-caste status, even though constitutional amendments had already been made to give them equal rights as citizens[24]. Racist ideology was later enacted with horrendous consequences during the Nazi period in Germany.

The only racist regime to have survived the Second World War and Cold War was the apartheid regime in South Africa. The apartheid laws which came into force not only prohibited intermarriage and sexual relations between Blacks and whites but also imposed strict segregation in residential areas for people of mixed race[25].

Perhaps evil seems too strong a word, but in the case of a government that was completely apathetic to the existence of other human beings, there is no better term than this. In early 2019 Belgium Prime Minister Charles Michel offered an apology for the kidnapping of thousands of children born to mixed race couples during colonial rule in Burundi, DR Congo and Rwanda. Mixed children born to Belgian settlers and local women were forcibly taken to Belgium and fostered by Catholic orders and other institutions. About 20,000 children were believed to have been affected in the 1940s and 1950s. They were taken to Belgium from 1956 until the independence of each of the three colonies. Some of the children were never granted Belgian citizenship and remained stateless. In the colonies, they were kept apart from White children. It was pure segregation[26]. I covered a lot on mixed marriages and biracial identity in my book 'Crossing the colour line: Mixed Marriage and Biracial Identity'.

18th century Europe had been the cradle of modern racism. The history of racism in Europe can provide clues as to why Nazi Germany wanted to eradicate an entire group of people, the Jews and Blacks. Racism annexed an important idea and movement in the 19th and 20th centuries and promised to protect each against all adversaries. European scientific accomplishments, a Puritan attitude toward life, a triumphant middle-class morality, Christian religion and the idea of beauty as a symbol of a better and healthier world were all integral aspects of racism[27].

Contemporary racial inequality has reproduced a new status quo which is more subtle, institutional and apparently non-racial. Racism in Europe has taken the approach of 'now you see it, now you do not'. For example, there is a lot of discrimination in the housing sector where covert behaviors in some countries offer accommodation to Black people in the same neighborhood, thereby segregating them from white majorities. Then locals star to complain of Black people creating ghettos or enclaves within their society.

In the labour sector, there is always the egregious form of discrimination. Black people are directed into menial jobs or allocating them jobs with little chance of mobility just to keep them in an inferior position. Even with two Masters degrees, it is common to find a Black person washing dishes in a restaurant, often working for many years without a promotion and with less remuneration than white colleagues with only high school diplomas.

The European Union Agency for Fundamental Rights (FRA) conducted a research study in 2018 on Being Black in the European Union (EU-MIDIS II).6,000 People of African Descent were interviewed in 12 member states; Austria, Denmark, Finland, France, Germany, Ireland, Italy, Luxembourg, Malta, Portugal, Sweden and the United Kingdom. The study revealed that People of African Descent experience an enormous amount of racism and discrimination in every sphere of life but particularly in racial profiling by the police. Even though profiling is an integral part of policing, when carried out with a bias motive, it makes it a racist and discriminative phenomenon. Almost one quarter (24%) of all persons of African Descent surveyed had been stopped by the police in the five years before the survey. Among these, 41% characterized the most recent stops as racial profiling. The study revealed that men are three times (22%) more likely to be stopped than women (7%). Respondents also rated their trust in the police as 6.3 on a scale of 0 to10[28].

The study also revealed that one third of the respondents (30%) reported having experienced racism in the five years before the survey; one fifth (21%) reported that they did so during the 12 months preceding the survey, yet only 14% of respondents had reported the most recent such incident to any authority. Experiences of racist harassment most commonly involve offensive non-verbal cues (22%) or offensive threatening comments (21%), followed by threats of violence (8%)[29].

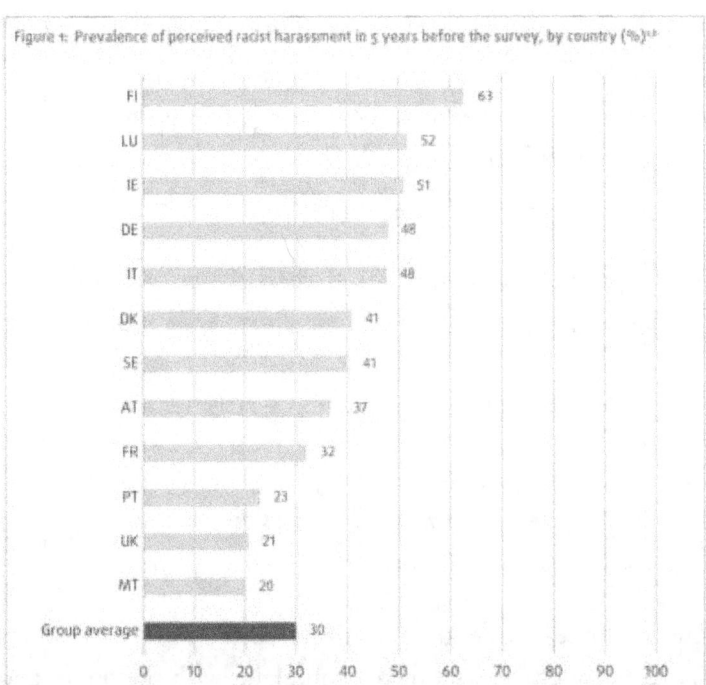

Figure 1: Prevalence of perceived racist harassment in 5 years before the survey, by country (%)[1,2]

FI	63
LU	52
IE	51
DE	48
IT	48
DK	41
SE	41
AT	37
FR	32
PT	23
UK	21
MT	20
Group average	30

SOURCE: FRA, EU-MIDIS II

LABOR MARKET PARTICIPATION is also not a level playing field and the findings exposed low-quality employment patterns that did not correspond to the level of education of applicants. The paid work-rate among those holding a tertiary degree is generally lower than that of the general population.

From those doing menial to professional jobs, racism in the workplace is a common phenomenon and can sometimes come from unexpected sources. Black doctors often face racism from their patients. Even though this does not happen in every

European country, there have been some recorded incidents and testimonies by victims. For example, a Nigerian doctor was the victim of hate speech while treating a patient in a hospital in Kozani, northern Greece. A 57-year old man told her 'you people need Hitler and some soap'[30].

A high-profile court case in the Netherlands was that of Jeffrey Koorndijk, a young Afro-Surinamese man who applied for an internship but accidentally received an email from the company he had applied to, containing racist remarks.

> *"I looked, it's nothing. First of all it is a dark colour nigger (neger). And on his résumé he has little experience with computers etc."*

An employee accidentally sent the email, intended for his manager, to Jeffrey, who filed a complaint with the police and shared it on Facebook[31].

Another challenge in the workplace is that of progression and retention. Again, based on systematic discrimination, it is hard for most People of African Descent to reach their full potential. Racism is codified in some corporate policies to the extent that it becomes a struggle to break a very real glass ceiling.

The findings in the housing sector are also worrying. They show that to a great extent, Persons of African Descent experience racial discrimination in access to private and public housing. Many also face precarious living conditions, which can exacerbate social exclusion.

The FRA survey report succinctly highlighted discriminatory practices in the housing sector across EU countries. In the report, one in five respondents of African Descent (21%) felt racially discriminated against in access to housing in the five years before the survey. The highest rates were observed in Italy and Austria (39% each) Luxembourg (36 %) and Germany (33 %). The lowest were observed in Denmark and the United Kingdom, where less than 10 % of respondents mentioned such experiences.

More than one in 10 respondents (14 %) of African descent say they were prevented from renting accommodation by a private landlord because of their racial or ethnic origin. The highest rates are observed in Austria (37 %), Italy (31 %), Luxembourg (28 %) and Germany (25 %). The lowest rate is observed in the United Kingdom (3 %). Some 6 % of respondents said that they were prevented from renting municipal/social housing because of their racial or ethnic origin.

Meanwhile, 5 % were asked to pay a higher rental rate because of their racial or ethnic origin, with respondents in Italy (20 %) and Austria (18 %) particularly affected[32].

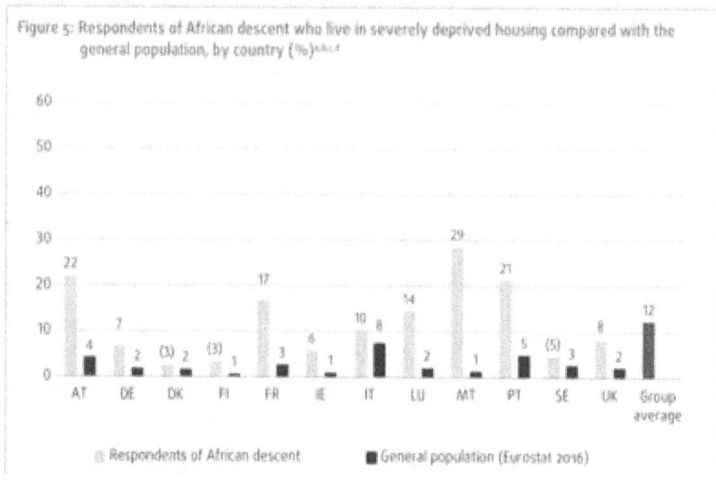

Figure 5: Respondents of African descent who live in severely deprived housing compared with the general population, by country (%)[a,b,c,d]

SOURCE: FRA, EU-MIDIS II

THE FINDINGS OF WORKING Group report of the UN High Commission Office for Human Rights on People of African Descent revealed the prevalence of discrimination in the housing and rental market. For example, Africans are often rejected by landlords once they hear an African accent or names over the phone[33]. This is something which is seen widely across Europe.

The Working Group report also exposed some disturbing racial discrimination in Belgium. In its Diversity Barometer: Housing, published in 2014, Unia, an independent public institution for combating discrimination and promoting equal opportunities, stated that landlords cited Moroccans and sub-Saharan Africans, among others, as being undesirable. This was often due to negative and incorrect stereotyping and prejudice, such as a belief that sub-Saharan Africans were lacking in hygiene. Furthermore, sub-Saharan Africans received explicitly racist and offensive statements from neighbours and landlords, which were linked to the negative image conveyed through the media and political discourse about Muslims and French-speaking Africans. The area of Belgium and the language spoken in that area also played a part. French-speaking Africans generally encountered particular difficulties in the Flemish-speaking region of Flanders.[34]

Racism in Classrooms

The education system is an existential instrument of knowledge transfer which functions across demographics. At school, children become endowed with the skills and mindset to navigate the environment they live in order to become contributing members of society. In addition to their parents' role, a child's literary world is of profound influence in their formative years. Children therefore merit an educational diet of diverse voices and viewpoints.

In stark contrast, both private and public schools across Europe are places of discrimination, victimization and harassment of children of African descent. Beginning in kindergarten all the way to university level, racism and discrimination are often rampant in educational institutions. This is racism perpetuated not only by students but also by some teachers.

Schools should provide a safe learning environment where children are nurtured to become responsible young people. Just as in a working environment, schools have an obligation to ensure that teachers, workers and students all adhere to the principle of non-discrimination. The tripartite linkage between school, parents and the community is essential in breaking these stereotypes and barriers.

The experiences of children and students of African descent from primary to tertiary education present a picture of meagre efforts aimed at fighting discrimination and racism. One aspect of this negligence is the inadequate provision of literary materials on African history as well as supportive roles for teachers and administrators.

There are numerous racist aspects of school life, ranging from discriminative treatment by teachers and peers to racist literary school materials, particularly prescribed textbooks with racial undertones. Taken together, these narratives contribute to the estrangement of black children. In fact, racism in European schools has been common for decades.

There are cases where teachers and the school administration are aware of a situation but they show a lack of attention to student fears, expectations and needs. The teachers' lack of interest in addressing student complaints serves to validate the incidents and reinforces racism within the school.

The use of the N-word and other insults blatantly directed against Black students is widespread in schools. These racial epithets append an already alienating educational system for many Black students.

In 2014, the university administration of Riga University in Latvia took disciplinary and educational measures following a complaint that a professor called a student of African descent a monkey-[35].

There are also cases where media outlets are complicit in perpetuating white supremacist thinking. It was appalling to watch a program for children outlining the purported benefits of colonialism in Africa aired on a Polish national TV station. These benefits include the promotion of European culture, values and languages and the stopping of cruel practices such as cannibalism. Such a program was cynically orchestrated with the full knowledge that there would be a backlash against people of African Descent. Unfortunately, these messages are being passed to a young generation who will grow up with this officially sanctioned mentality. Children are being conditioned into white race superiority even through the media.

Racism in Children's Books: The Paradox of Stories Meant to Nurture

Ten little nigger boys went out to dine;

One choked his little self, and then there were nine.

Nine little nigger boys sat up very late;

One overslept himself, and then there were eight.

Eight little nigger boys travelling in Devon;

One said he'd stay there, and then there were seven.

Seven little nigger boys chopping up sticks;

One chopped himself in half, and then there were six.

Six little nigger boys playing with a hive;

A bumble-bee stung one, and then there were five.

Five little nigger boys going in for law;

One got in chancery, and then there were four.

Four little nigger boys going out to sea;

A red herring swallowed one, and then there were three.

Three little nigger boys walking in the zoo;

A big bear hugged one, and then there were two.

Two little nigger boys sitting in the sun;

One got frizzled up, and then there was one.

One little nigger boy living all alone;

He got married, and then there were none[36].

As a parent, sharing a story with your children that was shared to you by your parents is one of those moments when you feel a strong sense of the power of inter-generational wisdom. Children always love bedtime stories, and this is complemented by their favourite books and some recommended from school. Some are also part of school curriculum and are required reading.

Children's books are laden with stories and illustrations and for years there have been elements of white superiority within the context in which words and stories are used. With the transitional change in the social climate, many of these stories and illustrations that were seen as benign have now been scrutinised for their dehumanizing, subjugating and prejudicial content; stories and illustrations which leave negative tropes in a child's mind. Such stories can be pernicious in their rendering of others who look physically different from them. Many parents, especially those of colour, are becoming weary of such reading-materials Sometimes, it is necessary to read the book a first time to check its content before reading it to a child, something which no parent should have to do.

Classical western literature has always been deficient of non-white characters and white supremacy has dominated the western literary canon for centuries. However, many non-western authors have been working actively to counter these particular narratives. Even though there is a much greater diversity in literature now, a lack of representation in some areas need to be addressed particularly with regard to the literary material aimed at young readers of colour. It is difficult to find children's stories or fairy tales with people of colour as the main characters. Rather, their inclusion will feature overt racial slurs, dehumanization and often a white saviour where Black people are mere character tropes facilitating white characters in gaining moral insights.

The more that Black characters are portrayed as weak, the further the white saviour concept is reinforced. White saviour books are inclined to give a negative picture of people of colour in which their fate is predicated upon white generosity. Thus, their inclusion services the needs and desires of white people. This underlying tenet of the white saviour phenomenon is widely covered in chapter three. Unfortunately, Europe's racist colonial policies are still present in school classrooms.

From The Story of Little Black Sambo (1899), The Story of Doctor Dolittle (1920) to Tin Tin in The Congo (1946), The Little Witch (1957) to Charlie and The Chocolate Factory (1964), these are just some of the better known children's books that are riddled with racial slurs and illustrations. Some of these books are featured in Annex Fig.1.

It is appalling to see how great European authors have gravitated towards projecting their white supremacist ideologies on to children who at a young age are unable to intellectualize their social realities. In effect, these children are being raised with the explicit notion of their racial superiority towards others and by extension, the other's racial inferiority. In these and other ways, many young people become sentient of the ideology of white supremacy. Their school libraries are stacked with books containing racial slurs. Until recently, most governments never thought of banning these kinds of books.

When I first came to Poland, I came across a poem, Murzynek Bambo (Negro Child) by Julian Tuwim (1934), which was then part of the school curriculum. 'Murzyn' is a contested word in Polish with a variety of interpretations. Most Poles say that it is not a derogatory word, mainly because they do not want to be perceived as racist. Most Africans detest this word because of its distinctly pejorative application in public discourse. The poem is about a Negro child, Bambo who is studious but when he comes home, he is mischievous, afraid to take a bath for fear of turning white. Throughout the poem, the plot is one in which the colour of Bambo's skin plays a central role. Even though it was banned in school curriculum a couple of years ago, the word 'murzyn' is still widely used to subordinate People of African Descent.

The context in which the narratives of these books are framed, are existential, hurtful, offensive and shameful. Even though most of the books are not laden with the N-word; they still reinforce racism and stereotypes that are hurtful to Black people and are a further reminder of their everyday realities. For Black schoolchildren, they have to put up with regular bombardments with racial slurs by white peers who have been conditioned to believing that they own the right to use the word. The fact that the words are written does not necessarily mean they have to be spoken. When a word such as the N-word that was previously a mandate for murder is present in a classroom, it has the potential to become a ticking-bomb. In fact, the Ku Klux Klan used the N-word when they were hanging, murdering, and shooting Black people in America.

Unfortunately, most white people ignore the usage of such racial slurs and often dismiss those who are advocating for their censorship as apologists for political correctness. The underlying question, is, are we going to allow our children to be bullied in classrooms, an environment where they should feel safe? Who are we protecting? Is it the oppressor or the oppressed?

Authors of colour have for a long time written many books about their respective communities even though few of these books reach the classrooms. If only white children were introduced to these books they could learn a lot about the bigotry that they have been nurtured on. They could begin to understand the deep-seated prejudices from the eyes of the oppressed. Similarly, white authors do not have to write books that put coloured communities on a secondary position, with stereotypical tropes. How hard is it to have literary materials with positive aspects of the coloured community without focusing entirely on their sufferings but their successes and achievements?

A paradigm shift is a fundamental requirement for streamlining policies on prejudice in school curricula. What is within the classroom is deciphered in the outside world and returns to the classroom having morphed into pervasive stereotypes. If White students can enjoy this largesse of learning about their humanity, coloured students should also be afforded such opportunities. Society functions best under these auspices.

Having said this, the big question we often ask is, should parents read racist books to their children? Whilst I would respect a parent who does not, I believe that children will always encounter a world of racism and prejudice, and it is the responsibility of the parent to help them navigate these challenges. Parents can play a central role by not censoring racist stories or illustrations but reading them and explaining the context in which they are used. By doing so, parents can disrupt and change the narrative. Children may be more prepared to listen and understand when they already know the words and their implications.

Beyond street attacks: Hate crime

WITH THE MUSHROOMING of Far-right wing, neo-fascist and neo-Nazi groups across Europe, there has been an exponential rise in attacks on People of African Descent and other minorities in several countries. Most of the attacks are racially motivated and therefore fall under the category of 'hate crime'.

Unfortunately, most governments do not have the proper mechanisms in place that would protect People of African Descent from physical attacks and discrimination. The lack of cogent frameworks and rigorous articulation of policies often leads to an aversion towards People of African Descent at both structural and societal level.

The EU's FRA has reported growing concerns regarding racist violence. According to their 2019 report on racist violence, 5 % of respondents say they have experienced a racist attack in the five years before the survey; 3 % say they did so during the 12 months before the survey. However, two thirds (64 %) of victims of racist violence, as well as a majority (63 %) of victims of racist physical attacks by police officers, did not report the most recent incident to any organisation – either because they felt reporting it would change nothing (34 %) or because victims do not trust or are afraid of the police (28 %).Whereas most victims (61 %) do not know the identity of the perpetrators, they generally identify them as not having a minority background (65 %). Some 38 % of victims identified perpetrators as having a minority ethnic background other than their own. One in 10 (11 %) of those who experienced racist violence say that a law enforcement officer was the perpetrator[37].

In 2017 in Dublin, Ireland, an African woman was violently attacked by an Irish woman. The same month, a Black man was killed by police at traffic-lights in London. In Germany, in the wake of the refugee crisis, it was reported that almost every day there were 10 attacks on people of colour. In the Netherlands in 2015 a group of Dutchmen in Woerden used eggs and fireworks to violently attack an asylum centre housing 150 refugees, including 50 children. Two years later, another Dutchman attacked a South African tourist while she checked out of her AirBnb accommodation in Amsterdam[38]. These are just a small number of examples of the violent attacks Black people face across Europe.

In June 2018, in Rosarno, an infamous Italian mafia stronghold, African migrant workers protested after three labourers were injured in a racially motivated shooting. Hundred of migrants were ordered to leave in what some commentators called 'ethnic cleansing'. One politician was even reported to have said that Rosarno had become the world's 'only white town'[39].

Still too few people are sufficiently conversant with the phenomenon of hate crime .In some ways, 'hate crime' is a misnomer, with the common perception that hate crime is about hate often being misleading. In fact, you do not need to hate someone to commit a crime. Hate is not a crime, but a state of emotions and hate crime is a message crime. It allows intolerance that was dormant to become articulated. The perpetrator singles out the victim upon identifying the victim's specific group under protected characteristics such as ethnicity, race, religion, sexual orientation and disability.

In a particular scenario where damage to possessions is involved, the property is targeted because of its affiliation with the individual or group and is likely to include targets such as places of worship, restaurants, homes or vehicles among others. The sad reality is that the majority of hate crime will never be addressed, never mind solved, but the message is still there.

One important element of hate crime is that unlike other forms of crime, hate crime has a greater impact on the victim. In fact, the psychological ramification is often dire for victims.

It is equally important to acknowledge that hate crime does not only affect the victim, but also the whole community associated with the victim. In addition to the fear of potential further attacks, psychological torture is a common phenomenon whereby the targeted community feels they were themselves the victims. This phenomenon can result in retaliatory and pre-emptive hate crime by victims.

In the absence of proper mechanisms and rigorous institutions for punishing perpetrators, the impact of hate crime on a society can be hugely detrimental. It creates perpetrator impunity, empowering others with a confidence to engage in such acts without fear of reprisal. This may also result in the resentment by victims towards law-enforcement agencies, the government and society at large, leading to further unreported incidents.

Even though People of African Descent widely experience hate crime compared to other minority communities in Europe, therein lies the fundamental problem of under-reporting. Under-reporting makes it difficult to gather statistics. When there is no reporting, there appears to be no crime in the picture. It is equally hard to deploy victim support mechanisms when under-reporting is commonplace and advocacy programs are stifled. Even though fingers may be pointed at victims for not reporting incidents there are a number of justified reasons that lead to under-reporting among People of African Descent across Europe. Some are based on their past experiences while others are based on the perceived notion of what may happen if they do report.

Many NGOs dealing with hate crimes work hard to eliminate the obstacles that lead victims to choose not to formally report hate crime incidents. Their work includes confidence-building by which victims and their families feel they are able to file a complaint without fear of dismissive treatment and/or reprisal and with the logical belief that doing so will render justice to them and their community at large.

However, there is still widespread apathy among People of African Descent to reporting incidents to the authorities. It is not enough for hate crimes to be recorded by authorities. Those who are targeted must also report incidents in order that the discourse might be normalised. Many victims do not come forward for a number of reasons and the victims remain invisible unless such incidents are reported and recorded. Here are some of the reasons why under-reporting is prevalent among People of African Descent across Europe;

Language barrier- In countries where English, German, Portuguese or French is not the lingua franca of most Black people; the local language becomes an impediment. Even though interpreters are at the disposal of victims in some countries should there be need, many interpreters do not feel sufficiently competent.

It is important to have competent interpreters who have been trained in the sensitivities of the interview process and can be trusted to reflect the actual words of the interviewee. Some of these interpreters are also biased and interpret in a manner that provides little tangible evidence.

Mistrust in authorities- Hate crime goes unreported because victims and affected communities are lacking in trust, especially after previous experiences of deaths in police custody, profiling on streets and extrajudicial killings. Black people believe the police will do little especially after listening to the stories of other victims. The choices the police make when conducting an investigation also play an essential role. If a victim reports that he or she is a victim of hate crime and the police do not ask a particular question to prove that point, it will not be part of the investigation. There have also been cases where the victims are re-victimised. In this case, it is hard for the victim to trust the process and he/she will be discouraged from making any follow-up.

The lack of trust Black people have towards the police stems from current systematic and historical abuses sometimes based on their previous experiences with the police in their countries of origin. The failure of the legal system in rendering justice to victims of hate crime is attributable to the systematic police dysfunction to investigate and prosecute perpetrators. This can partly be attributed to lack of training and (or) their aversion to

Black people; some police officers are also white supremacists and exhibit racist tendencies.

In some cases, the victim becomes the perpetrator particularly when the victim is Black. One example is that of a Hungarian student of Nigerian descent visiting Malta where he was spat at and slapped by a white woman at a bus terminal. At the time of the incident the police used force to arrest the Nigerian victim. The Maltese police officers and government officials later apologised for the way the Nigerian had been treated[40]. This kind of experience reflects Black people's reluctances to report hate crime cases to the police because of the way they would be treated and victimised.

Fear of dismissive treatment and reprisals: Victims often live in fear of retaliation especially when the perpetrator is known to the victim, most especially when the perpetrator is a neighbour. In fact, some hate crime incidents involve people known to the victim.

Intersectionality is also an essential element in understanding the impact of hate crime across demographics. Being cognizant of how men and women are differently affected by hate crime can be instrumental in planning victim support services and prevention programs. The mainstreaming of gender into hate crime data collection mechanisms is ultimately important.The role of disaggregated data in the prevention and response to hate crime is potentially enormous.

Certain types of hate crime may be more commonly committed against men as compared to women and vice versa.

For example, men may be more likely to be victims of physical assaults whereas women may be more likely to be targets of sexual violence.

Police Violence

Unfortunately, those who are mandated with the responsibility to serve and protect can at the same time be the perpetrators of crime against Black people.

Across Europe, Black people are susceptible to police violence. This often starts with racial profiling, and then physical attacks ensue. Police violence is itself a corollary to police racial profiling. Even though racial profiling is part of policing, when motivated by bias it becomes a racist act. For many years, the police and other law enforcement agents have systematically failed to protect Black people from violence against white supremacists, neo-Nazis and neo-Fascists.

According to ENAR, the European Network Against Racism, statistics, between 2004 and 2014, 509 people from Black, refugee and migrant communities died under suspicious circumstances where the police, prison authorities or immigration detention officers have been implicated[41].

One typical case which fits the symbiotic connection between police profiling and violence occurred in Cyprus when a refugee from the Ivory Coast was stopped by police at immigration control. The police officer resorted to force when an altercation ensued between him and the refugee, breaking his leg during the process. Even though there was a video recording of the entire incident, the Ivorian was instead charged for causing bodily harm to the police officer[42].

The police mishandling of Black people stirs memories of the highly publicised inquiry into the death of teenager Stephen Lawrence who was murdered by a group of up to six white youths in a racially motivated attack in London in 1993. Stevens' murder inquiry sparked a discourse on policing and racism and should have been a clarion call for law enforcement agencies to review their policies on dealing with minorities. However, institutional racism continues to be part of the everyday experience of minorities. A 350-page report concluded that the investigation into the murder of Stephen Lawrence was flawed by the amalgamation of 'professional incompetence, institutional racism and a failure of leadership'[43]. Annex, Fig. 4, is a list of cases of Black people who have died in police custody in the UK.

In May 2010, in Poland, during a police-raid of the Stadium open-air market in Warsaw, a Nigerian trader was targeted. As police handcuffed him, one of his friends, Maxwell Itoya approached them to ask what was going on. Itoya spoke Polish so he thought he could help. Within a split second, a police-officer shot him at point blank range. Maxwell bled to death before an ambulance arrived on the scene. After two years of investigations, the prosecutor discontinued the proceedings in the case citing a lack of circumstantial evidence[44]. Maxwell Itoya's death left his three children fatherless.

In Germany, the case of Sierra Leonean, Oury Jalloh, has been dragging on for over 14 years and has shown the brutality of the police. Oury was an asylum seeker who died in police custody in the eastern state of Saxoy-Anhalt in 2005. His severely burnt body was found with hands and feet tied to a mattress even though at that time, he was alone in his cell.

According to new documents revealed by the German public broadcaster WDR, in 2017, it was found that he could not have set himself on fire. Experts on fire safety, medicine and chemistry all concluded that Jalloh's death was more likely to have been caused by someone else, a direct contradiction of police claims that the 36-year old had committed suicide[45].

These are just a few examples of the Black people who have succumbed to police brutality. There remains a vast number of police killings and unresolved cases across Europe.

According to the FRA survey report, the rate of police stops and perceived racial profiling varies substantially between countries. In both periods (5 years and 12 months before the survey), respondents were stopped most often in Austria (5yrs: 66%, 12 months: 39%) and Finland (5 years: 38%, 12 months: 22%). However, in Austria, the rate at which the most recent police stop was perceived as ethnic profiling is almost 8 times higher than that in Finland (31% vs. 4%) when looking at the 12 months before the survey. Men are three times more likely to be stopped than women (22% vs. 7%) and four times more likely to perceive the most recent stop as racial profiling (men: 17%, women: 4%).

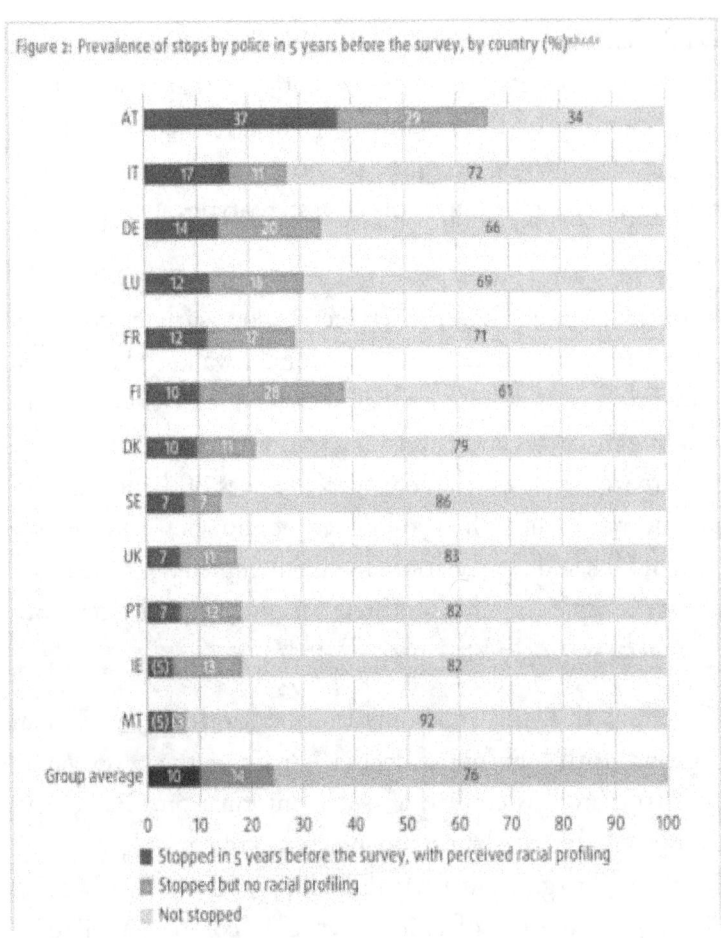

Figure 2: Prevalence of stops by police in 5 years before the survey, by country (%)

- ■ Stopped in 5 years before the survey, with perceived racial profiling
- ▨ Stopped but no racial profiling
- ▨ Not stopped

Source: FRA, EU-MIDIS II

The Stereotypes Conundrum

THROUGHOUT MY TIME in Europe, I have met a vast number of white people who have visited countries in Africa.

Whilst engaging in conversation with them, it dawns on me that they possess varying perceptions that show their understanding of the continent is misinformed. The single story phenomenon becomes so pronounced that it leaves nothing but a whole bunch of racial stereotypes.

Africa as a victim is well projected trope particularly within the white saviour complex. Africa is seen as poor with the common sights of malnourished children, women walking half naked with buckets of water on their heads, disease-ridden locals wielding machetes and gun-toting warlords; a continent where the largesse of donors has changed the lives of dying children and mothers; where their rolling tears of hopelessness are now tears of bliss and appreciation. I will talk more about the white saviour complex in Chapter three. Meanwhile, let us look into how racial stereotypes are perpetuated.

We know that the mass media loves nothing more than negative stories. European media is part of the propaganda infrastructure disseminating such information. Bad news always sells better than good news regardless of geography. People tend to gravitate towards bad news particularly because they find some sort of relief when they compare their own situation to perhaps the dire situation of others. In so doing they benefit from other's misery. Europeans struggling with paying a mortgage may feel better by watching the news of people in Africa surviving without water, electricity and little food. This phenomenon was shown recently when the UK's The Sun newspaper ran a story about a mother who, allegedly tired of listening to her daughters' relentless moaning about how poor they thought they were, took them on a trip to

Uganda (a country where some children do not have shoes or toys).[46]

This mother said that the unconventional holiday was mind-blowing for her children. She said the reason for taking the trip was that her children were always complaining that they were poor while their friends could afford holidays, Xbox's etc. Taking them to Uganda was a way of showing them that there are poorer people in the world and that that should make them feel better.

The negative portrayal of Africa in European media resonates with the realities of the stereotyping they face in everyday life. Many Africans feel strongly about the way Africa is portrayed in the western media and indeed western journalists have often been accused of racial stereotyping African coverage. Many Africans in the Diaspora are even more cognizant of these negative perceptions because their life is dependent on how locals perceive them through the prism of the media.

It is very common for white people to attribute characteristics of a one Black person based on the one other Black person they have interacted with or heard of. One Black person therefore becomes the representative of an entire Black community. However, you will never find a white person attributing a character of one white person to the entire white community.

Living in a country with many paedophile cases ranging from Catholic priests to locals, I have never heard anybody deeming Poland a paedophile country, even though this is what reality shows. We cannot designate Poland a paedophile country by virtue of having a certain percentage of paedophiles. Then what can be the rationale in generalising about Africa when there is an outbreak of any case possible be it Ebola, conflicts, Aids etc.? Well of course we know that it is the racial stereotype mentality embedded within the parameters of white supremacy that creates these projections.

A stereotype is a cognitive construct which allows your brain to make a snap judgment on directly visible characteristics such as gender, race, religion, disability. Our brain is hard-wired to make quick calls, and that is natural. The problem emerges when we begin to employ those stereotypes over and above that instant impulse. This is called 'bias' and is essentially a conviction that a stereotype is factual. For example, the stereotype that women are bad drivers could lead to the implication that an inherent biological difference between women and men constitutes this divergence.

Sometimes racial stereotyping is less scary and more just plain embarrassing. I could be walking along, minding my own business when the inevitable happens. Someone (it is always a white person) asks me for marijuana, asks me if I speak African or may sometimes even touches my hair or skin and wonder why my skin is not hairy. Some comments are just absurd.

Why do we then form these racial stereotypes? A rational answer to this question is that we learn from our parents, friends and from the media, with the media re-enforcing these stereotypes. People like, want and need to classify both the social and physical world into small clusters. Once you have made your classification, you have no business in reflecting on an individual member of a group and you can continue to generalize group information.

The question is, why do we do this? Why do we choose this path? Well, we do it for some simple reasons.

First, we do not know how to engage with people who belong to that different group. So if you have already had interactions with Africans, you will notice that Black people are not monolithic but diverse and next time you meet a Black person, you will be less likely to generalize. Because of the diversity of the African disapora communities, people do not necessarily have experience dealing with different ethnic groups, therefore, people generalize and stereotype based on preconceived notions.

The second reason is that the media reinforces stereotypes. When we hear of a terrorist attack in Sweden or in Britain, you often hear the media associate it immediately with Muslims. We therefore begin to think that the whole Muslim community thinks and behaves in the same way. The third reason is that we are lazy or reluctant to go beyond our comfort zones and dig deeper into knowing and understanding individuals that are members of a particular group. So we tend to generalize and stereotype.

In the role of race and racial prejudice, and in recognizing other people, John Brigham explains that, we are faced with an existential challenge when asked to recognize individuals, distinguish them from each other and to treat each individual appropriately. If one is unable to distinguish members of a particular group from each other, then it is difficult to treat each person with the individuality that he or she deserves. Failing to treat a person as a unique individual is often seen as a central characteristic of stereotyping and prejudice. There are many things that can interfere with one's motivation or ability to treat others as individuals. Group membership is one such factor. Researchers have identified the out-group homogeneity effect, the finding that people in out groups are seen as more homogenous, more similar to each other, than are members of one's own group. The out-group homogeneity effect stems from the idea that because they are classified as a group, members of group must all be alike. People tend to see their own group as a heterogeneous set of unique individuals, while out groups, as a set of similar individuals persons. This is exactly what happens with race categorization[47].

Africa for instance, based on phenotypical characteristics across the continent, is often considered to be homogeneous, characterizing all Africans as Black with similar facial features. As anthropologists have detailed, Africa holds the majority of physical and genetic variation on the planet. It has the shortest and the tallest people, populations with the thickest and thinnest lips, very wide differences in width of noses and skull dimensions, different shades of skin color from light brown to a very much darker color; nose shape from flat to aquiline; and hair color as well[48].

Genetic studies in Africa show continuous shades of gene frequencies between populations thought to be single 'tribes', as well as genetic similarities between populations thought to be biologically very separate. Indeed, the existence of distinct tribes in Africa has often been traced to arbitrary and convenient administrative and political divisions made by colonial masters[49].

Stereotypes matter because they are part and parcel of everyday life. They influence our judgments and behavior towards other individuals, often entirely in ways that we are unaware of. These stereotypes become part of our everyday language. And these behaviors create self-fulfilling prophecies that bring out the stereotypes in their targets. They are the cognitive monsters that poison many of our social interactions. We are particularly likely to stereotype people we do not know very well or we do not care about.

In short, we may use our stereotypes almost exclusively when the category is all the information we have about someone, or if we are not particularly interested in getting to know the person any better.

We are a lot more likely to categorize people using categories that are perpetually salient. As a result, categorization occurs frequently on the basis of people's sex, race, age, and physical attractiveness, in part because these traits are immediately physically apparent to us when we see other people[50].

A Paradigm Shift

What can we do collectively to combat stereotypes? I believe that there is still hope. There are things one can do to prevent and respond to stereotypes;

Be honest with yourself and acknowledge that you intrinsically have these biases. It's ok. It is the next step you take that counts. These steps should be geared towards correcting your biases by being aware that they play a role in your life. If you are a teacher, are biases influencing how you assess and advise students. Parents, are you sending the wrong message to your children? If you are a witness, are you ready to react or give viable information to the police? We are all part of this problem in one way or the other. The next step we take determines whether continue to encourage it or prevent it from escalating.

Get out of your comfort zone. Try to know more about people who are different from you or how the stereotypes came into to effect.

Tolerance, especially cultural tolerance can also be the answer. Once you recognize that and stop looking at other cultures only through your own lenses, you may understand how stereotypes came about and eventually come to terms with thinking about remedies.

An equally important point is that whenever you are interacting with someone you consider different from you, try to find one common thing with that person. I promise you, you will find that you have more in common than the differences. Skin colour is just superficial, deep inside, we are pretty much the same.

And the last point is that, whenever you interact with someone you consider different, get to know them as an individual not as a group. By doing so, you are less likely to stereotype the entire community.

Afrophobia: Anti-Black sentiments

PEOPLE OF AFRICAN DESCENT are one of the largest marginalized groups in Europe comprising approximately 15 out of 508 million people. This makes Black Europeans one of the largest minority groups on the continent. This community of African Descent ranges from recent migrants to generations who were born in Europe[51].

However, their common experience is based on discriminatory and stigmatizing practices due to their physical attributes, colour, nationality and immigration status.

But as is the case for other visible minorities such as Roma and Muslims citizens (of which Black people also make up a significant proportion), they experience the highest levels of socio-economic exclusion, negative stereotyping and acts of violence.

Even though the United Nations Commissioner for Human Rights on People of African Descent and the European Union have already provided recommendations for discrimination and recognition of the challenges the African community face, especially with regard to structural racism and discrimination, national legislatures still lack robust policies for countering Afrophobia both at a structural and societal level.

According to the FRA, migration policies at both EU and national levels are entrenched in institutional racism, hierarchizing workers in relation to inherent racialised criteria such as expatriates, low/medium or high skilled workers, students, researchers, family reunification migrants, seasonal migrants, circular migration migrants, blue card migrants, refugees, asylum seekers, subsidiary protection beneficiaries among others. Every category of migrants receives a limited and unequal set of rights in relation to labour market engagement, democratic participation, and access to housing, services, healthcare etc[52].

Afrophobia involves sentiments that are centred around the perceived notions that Africans are uncivilized.

These negativities often project fear, antagonism and disdain. Afrophobia is built within the premise of discrimination based on a person's skin colour, nationality, and ethnic origin. Other phobias such as Islamophobia and homophobia involve the subjugation and dehumanizing of a group of people and deny them their fundamental human rights as outlined within the universal declaration of human rights.

Afrophobia in its entirety is also compounded further by the intersectionality that encompasses homophobia, Islamophobia and other projected characteristics such as disability, religion and sex. Afrophobia takes different dimensions and often entails hate crime and hate speech against People of African Descent.

Carol Anderson in her book 'White Rage' posits that "the trigger for white rage, inevitably, is Black advancement. It is not the mere presence of Black people that is the problem; rather, it is Blackness with ambition, with drive, with purpose, with aspirations and with demands for full and equal citizenship. It is Blackness that refuses to accept subjugation, to give up[53].

This is particularly valid and apparent in Europe. Well educated, intelligent and successful Africans often face scrutiny of their educational and financial backgrounds. Sometimes there are derogatory remarks about how Europe has helped them reach their position even though their fellow Africans are a lazy lot. An African in a higher position is a threat to many white colleagues and this is the reason why there is a reinforced glass ceiling for Africans in the labour market.

Afrophobia can sometimes take a different trajectory, becoming more egregious in the form of hate crime and hate speech. This happens in different countries. There is no single country in Europe where a Black person has never been physically assaulted because of the colour of their skin. An example from Sweden involves Somali woman and her children attacked in the small town of Tomelilla. The attackers shouted insults such as 'fucking negro', 'take off the curtain (veil) from your face' at the woman. The perpetrators also threw stones at them hitting the woman whilst she was protecting her children[54].

In Belgium, Cécile Djunga, a weather presenter of African descent with Radio-Télévision Belge de la Communauté Française, posted an online video in 2018, saying that she had been a victim of hate speech including comments that she was "too black and all people could see were her clothes". The video evoked a national discourse with a call for diversity in the media especially among presenters.[55]

It is an appalling fact that Afrophobia is prevalent in every aspect of life and across all demographics.

CHAPTER TWO

Race: The Dark Side of Europe

LOCATED ON THE NORTH bank of the Tagus River in Portugal, stands the gigantic, much celebrated Discovery monument erected in 1960 to commemorate the 500th anniversary of the death of Prince Henry the Navigator. It features 33 prominent people of that time. It towers 52 meters above the water, in the only European capital on the Atlantic Ocean. The monument celebrates Portugal's heroes and pioneers who sailed across the Atlantic to amass the wealth of the 'New World' which would be critical to the development of both Portugal and the rest of Europe. These pioneers made the perilous journey across the Atlantic to conquer the world on the basis of opening up trade-routes.

As tourists from many countries and walks of life flock to admire the Discovery monument, many are oblivious of the murderous history behind these celebrated individuals. Many of them do not know that the wealth and prestige they are admiring came as a result of a slave trade that cost the lives of a huge number of people.

The Transatlantic slave trade (also known as the Middle Passage) was different from other slave trades such as the trans-Saharan trade in the sense that it created the concept of race. The colonialists and slave traders used physical geographical features to demarcate their subjects in Africa, drawing boundaries between African kingdoms and creating new states in their own interest. And it is these boundaries that have posed huge land problems in modern Africa.

Race became part of the arsenal for acquiescence and was used to legitimise African inferiority by white masters. The dynamic of this racial construct is practised to this day. . And we can see how significant Transatlantic slavery was to the construction of race. When Black slaves were shipped across the Atlantic, they were rendered a servile mass, people without names and without culture. Slave masters then gave them new names, erasing their history.

It is clear that racism existed prior to the Transatlantic slave trade and in fact, it is upon a history of racism that slavery was founded. Race and slavery became the foundations of colonialism. To enslave an individual, an aspect of 'otherness' had to be created using skin colour and religion to subjugate, a tool used to rationalize white superiority. Even though slavery was officially abolished in the 19th century, the racial hierarchies present today are premised on the history of slavery. A history which sees the Transatlantic slave trade presented as a natural legacy.

Race is a ubiquitous social construct conceptualized by scientists, historians and philosophers to validate racial inequity and to safeguard white dominance over others. Given that race is a social construct, whoever is characterized as white will vary depending on their heritage.

Since race is the creation of social impetus, it has been patented along class lines. In a society that provides little to those who are non-white, economic and racial impetus can be seen to complement one another.

Swayed by European travel documentaries, colonial films and white philosophers, anthropologists, ethnographers, and fiction writers in the eighteenth and nineteenth centuries, the West came to understand non-whites as inferior others. More specifically the construction of whiteness functioned epistemologically and ontologically as a prism through which the 'other' was constructed and rendered subhuman [56]

The great chain of being became an ordering in a hierarchical structure in an age when the West was possessed by fervour for scientific discovery and exploration. It served as a powerful means of organizing the natural world; the 'Other' was seen as a part of the chaotic and exotic natural landscape in need of being ordered, properly identified, categorized and subdued by those whites who thought of themselves as the very expressions of a teleological order that privileged whiteness as the quintessence of beauty, intelligence, and cultural and historical progress[57].

I believe the majority of people have understood race as a biological and genetic variation among different races. This biological understanding of race is categorically embedded in the differences in physiological attributes such as skin color, hair texture, nose and lip shape and other characteristics such as sexual aptitude or physical ability. For those who subscribe to race as a biological construct, the difference in races is something natural. Whereas in fact we now know that the physical differences we see such as hair texture and eye color, are superficial and emerged as adaptations to geography[58].

The external, physical characteristics that have been used to define race are unreliable indicators of genetic variation between any two people[59]. Nonetheless, there remains a stubborn conviction that the variation connected with race is innate. In order to demystify the myth of race as a biological construct, we should recognize the social and economic interests that propelled science into categorizing society and its chattel along racial lines.

That European society is profoundly disconnected and asymmetrical in terms of race and whiteness is the legacy of this bogus, lopsided logic. By this logic, white people become shielded from racial pressure, are convinced they are unconstrained by it and in addition are justified in being able to benefit from it. It is difficult to imagine how any white person could say that they are subjected to racial distress, given that they exist in a society where they are the dominant group. White people often therefore see the challenging of their global racial views as a challenge to their own identity as good and decent people[60].

They consider any intervention which links them to the structure of racism, a disconcerting and inequitable ethical felony. The sheer mention that being white has some significance often elicits an array of opposing reactions. As Robin DiAngelo wrote in her book 'White Fragility', these reactions can include emotions such as anger, fear, guilt and behaviors such as argumentation, silence and withdrawal from the stress-inducing situation. For these very reasons, D'Angelo coined the concept of white fragility which she correlates with discomfort and anxiety, born of superiority and entitlement. White fragility is widely covered in Chapter Three.

These days, in addition to members of white supremacist organizations, only a tiny percentage of white people profess to being racists, whilst in reality, it is difficult to find a normal, white person professing to be racist. Many white people resort to colour blind ideology stating that they only see people, that even though racism still exists, it does not play a significant role in shaping Black people's future.

On the contrary, as Bonilla-Silver[61] contends, most whites insist that minorities especially Blacks are the ones responsible for whatever race problem they have in America. They publicly denounce Blacks for playing the race card, for demanding the maintenance of unnecessary and divisive race-based programs, such as affirmative action, and for crying racism whenever they are criticized by white folks.

Most whites believe that if Black folks and other minorities would just stop thinking about the past, work hard, and complain less (particularly about racial discrimination) then Europeans of all hues could all get along.

The horrendous misfortunes of slavery that overshadow Europe's past have left an indelible mark on the lives of millions of men and women. It imposed upon European societies a wave of prejudice and disparity in every aspect of life. Unfortunately, at present, its repercussions are being dismissed through the vehicle of racial stereotyping.

Race and Ethnicity in the Bible

*Slaves, obey your earthly masters with respect and fear and with sincerity of heart, just as you would obey Christ...***Ephesians 6:5**

'When the missionaries arrived, the African had the land and the missionaries had the Bible. They taught us how to pray with our eyes closed. When we opened them, they had the land and we had the Bible' ... **Jomo Kenyatta, the First President of the Republic of Kenya (Facing Mount Kenya)**

Prejudice is as old as humanity. Christianity, a religion that transformed Africa during colonialism had its share of surprises. Prejudice was as prevalent during the times of the Old and New Testaments as it is now. Both worlds had diverse cultures, languages and traditions. Just as we have the locals and outsiders today, the ancient people had the same. There were enemies as well as friends. Prejudice existed in a wide array of areas, as it does now.

During colonialism, most schools were turned into prisons and Africans had little access to books and education, as the colonialists believed the indigenous population would become empowered and revolt. They had to be kept in a state of servitude. The Bible became the most revered book of all time. Africans adopted Christianity, abandoning their traditional religions and spirituality. Churches and the Bible became a source of refuge at a time when the very people who brought the Bible were raping, killing, and torturing locals. It is fact that the Bible is more widely read in Africa than any other book. Many Africans know more about the Bible than they do about their own culture and traditions.

Before the missionaries, alias the colonialists, conquered Africa, the continent was widely practising African spirituality which was central to the lives of most Africans. Our values and morals were embedded within the norms of African spirituality. African spirituality was practised across different regions and formed transnational linkages. Colonialism destroyed these linkages disrupting the spirit of *Ubuntu, harambee, ujamaa* with fundamental moral and spiritual consequences. The connection with the sun, the mountains, the lakes and rivers defined our existence before the coming of missionaries.

Ali Mazrui in his book, *Shifting Identities* noted that among the most serious consequences of colonial rule and racial domination are the crises of identity which they generate. The old assurances of long-established traditional identities are suddenly shaken[62]. He goes on to mention that, in most parts of Africa there was no such thing as a Christian identity before the arrival of the white man and his cultural baggage. Christianity was not only the propagation of a new religion, it was also the creation of a new identity in sharp contrast to say, African Muslim identity or traditional religious identity.

Skin colour, ethnicity, and language became an integral channel for prejudice. This is evidenced in some scriptures in the Bible that still leave us with questions as to what were the consequences. These may be contested by ardent supporters. Consider these examples;

Even though the term race was not used in the Bible, as far as I understand the Bible, some form of categorization such as tribe was widely imputed in order to create hierarchy, for instance;

In the book of Numbers 36:8, the daughters throughout the tribe of Israel who are in line to inherit property must marry within their tribe, so that all the tribe will keep their ancestral property.

The Bible is also heavily laden with ethnic prejudice;

Deuteronomy 17:14-15 14. "You are about to enter the land the Lord your God is giving you. When you take it over and settle there, you may think, 'We should select a king to rule over us like the other nations around us.' 15. If this happens, be sure to select as king the man the Lord your God chooses. You must appoint a fellow Israelite; he may not be a foreigner.

Even though ethnicity or race is not strongly used here, it is obvious that there existed a superiority complex. One prominent similarity here is the modus operandi of the missionaries, alias colonialists. Their process of converting Africans to Christianity was a strategy which pushed Africans into servitude.

Exodus 34:11-13. But listen carefully to everything I command you today. Then I will go ahead of you and drive out the Amorites, Canaanites, Hittites, Perizzites, Hivites, and Jebusites. 12. "Be very careful never to make a treaty with the people who live in the land where you are going. If you do, you will follow their evil ways and be trapped.. Instead, you must break down their pagan altars, smash their sacred pillars, and cut down their Asherah poles.

Sometimes, the ethnic stratification in the Bible is more obvious. Here again, in this chapter, ethnic relations are highlighted and the idea of mixed marriage denounced.

New Testament, Ezra 9:1-2 *1. When these things had been done, the Jewish leaders came to me and said, "Many of the people of Israel and even some of the priests and Levites, have not kept themselves separate from the other peoples living in the land. They have taken up the detestable practices of the Canaanites, Hittites, Perizzites, Jebusites, Ammonites, Moabites, Egyptians, and Amorites. 2. For the men of Israel have married women from these people and have taken them as wives for their sons. So the holy race has become polluted by these mixed marriages.*

Christianity and Islam at some point are myopic in Africa. Nigeria (Africa's largest country in terms of population) and Sudan(Africa's largest country in terms of territory) serve as a case study. In Nigeria, almost all Hausa are Muslims; almost all Igbo are Christians; and Yoruba are split between Christians and Muslims. Islam has perpetuated Hausa identity distinguishing them from other non-Muslim groups; Christianity has perpetuated Igbo identity while Yoruba are split between Christians and Muslims. It is unequivocal that the Hausa, Igbo and Yoruba would not have felt more or less culturally superior had their respective identities not been Islamised or Christianised.

Even though Christianity and Islam are universal religions in terms of their underlying tenets, their adaptation in Africa undoubtedly had repercussions. Sudan (now Sudan and Southern Sudan) also serve as a good example. Southern Sudan is non-Muslim while the northern part is Islamised and Arabised. The rift between the north and south has been widened by 1 Christian minority leaders. It is apparent that Christianity and Islam resulted in aggravating regional and ethnic sectionalism[63].

Navigating the Discourse on Race

A CONVERSATION ON STRUCTURAL racism, white privilege, white supremacy and prejudice can escalate quite quickly . New and distinct emotional hardwiring and infrastructures are needed in an issue that has historical connections, plays a central role in a modern, global society and is of paramount importance. We have seen on TV or in conferences when people become enraged during debates on race and racism, which expose their biases and fragilities. We have heard white folk deliberately saying Black folk are becoming racist the more that they talk about racism, trying to silence them. Can Black people be racist? Well, I hold a nuanced and distinct view. Racism is about power dynamics. Black people have no institutions that subjugate other races, Black people do not feel superior because they are Black and Black people do not have the privileges which come with skin colour. Racism is about holding the power that makes one race feel superior to other races. Racism is about creating structures that benefit its creators.

Talking about race or white privilege should not automatically lead to an argument. The basic requirement of rationality is an imperative. There are ways to achieve this, depending on the preparedness of parties in the discussion; it demands a greater sense of awareness and deep understanding of the topic based both on historical facts and unfolding current events. White violence is perpetuated by the easy budget of silence. Silence justifies racist acts which prompts the escalation of racist incidents. The big question that lingers is how can one engage in the race discourse without starting an argument? How could you predict the response of the receiving party?

Knowing who might be prepared to lend an ear could be tricky and very unpredictable. Choosing the right time and the right place to engage in a conversation could provide an effective antidote. For many people, there is neither a right time nor right place; any place is a free space to engage in the discourse. This could however, pose a problem. The environment in which we talk is fundamental and constantly shifting depending on various other forces that play a central role. Here are some ideas for turning a difficult conversation into a productive one.

Capturing an audience

Understanding the objectives in terms of why you need to engage in the conversation is an essential element; for instance, who is the target group? What do we want to achieve? And are we well conversant with the reality that could leverage such discussion and engagement?

Understanding the target audience

It is easier to know the current state of affairs if one knows what is on the menu. It is then much easier to place an order, otherwise you might order what is not being served. Understanding this and by engaging in the conversation with the person at the receiving end amounts to changing the narrative. It could be a perception or demystifying certain myths. Therefore keeping abreast of what sources of information can be used plays a significant role here. Counter-narratives go beyond providing this information and can lead to empowerment and awareness raising.

Talking from a vantage point

It is important to discuss the narratives from the vantage point of the affected community. Discussing counter-narratives can propel others into understanding how things work from the other side. Giving people something to think about might precipitate questions that normally go unasked. Conveying how a situation affects those who are vulnerable and what we can do collectively to utilise the situation is also important. It may precipitate empathy among the people who feel more invested in the normative narrative. Questioning the status quo and finding common ground on how to reach a conclusive and objective resolution could heighten the awareness of a need for collective responsibility.

Shared values

Starting conversation with shared human values could, to an extent generate empathy on the subject. For instance, discussing how racism affects our shared values, mentioning that we share more in common than our differences could be a starting point. Beginning a conversation with issues on shared values could encourage the listener to understand what makes us the same rather than different. Engaging in a dialogue as tough and sensitive as race requires a tactical approach. Applying rhetoric to trigger emotional empathy could provide opportunities for further discussion and active engagement.

Building bridges

I suggest starting a conversation with shared values and proceeding to the opportunities that can arise should those shared values be respected. Creating a nexus of shared values with equity and inclusion can trigger the listener into rethinking the next action needed and how to achieve it.

Having a discussion based on shared values can be a good icebreaker. People understand better when they identify and understand shared common values. It can show that we are more connected than we are different. Showing the narrative that we are all equal in some way or the other could be a good start.

Providing the way forward

Providing a solution rather than the cause could appeal to many people. Providing the best way you believe could be a good way to unite people rather than saying things that might lead to a blame game. Solutions or recommendations always appeal to many people. It means one is focused upon reaching an end rather than focusing on the means.

Having engaged in building a strong starting point, it is time to move further into providing a solution. Many people believe that there is nothing that can be done about racism and that it will never end. Providing a solution could be a better game-changer. Starting with the root cause of the problem, then describing it and its consequences before moving to potential solutions could trigger some hopeful thinking.

Addressing Systemic Impediments

Engaging in a discussion on how structural racism impacts the affected community could also have leverage. We all know the ramifications of inequality and racial injustices; the effect of systemic racism on Black people. Putting these issues at the forefront could precipitate a productive discussion rather than talking about how the system is failing.. Many White people do not understand what Black people experience internally, even though might have contact with Black people. One has to be Black to fully understand the experience of course. Vividly and honestly telling people what it actually means to be Black is one way of breaking down barriers. Many White people do not understand structural racism and there is a denial that comes from not acknowledging the structural part of racism. It is imperative to educate White people on the consequences of structural racism and how it affects us all.

To paraphrase from Peter Tosh's 1977 song, 'everyone is praying for peace but no one is praying for justice.' It is very common for people to look at racism as a people-driven phenomenon and so it is scrutinised at a micro-level. It is obvious that racism began with individuals and that as the group became larger, racism became institutionalized. This is the reason that the issue of race has become such a big subject now due to its omnipresence at both the individual and institutional level. For instance, when we engage in a discussion of the inequality between Blacks and whites in Europe, it would be highly relevant to include the processes of slavery, colonialism and its outcomes, especially in education, the labor market etc., and linking it to the current situation.

Over time, the narrative that Black people are not economically empowered because they are intrinsically lazy has become common thinking. It is of course, like saying that Black people are naturally predisposed to being lazy. Talking about the history of institutional racism does not mean you need to go through the chronology of events. Establishing equilibrium against the background of the problem and how it led to the current state of affairs is equally significant.

Moving Forward Together

It may be more appropriate to discuss how prejudice and discrimination hold us all back. Discussing collective responsibility and appropriate action may be more effective than the blame game.

Having mentioned the negative impact of racism and discrimination, it is equally important to tackle issues related to systematic prejudices and their consequences. It is prudent to explain how systematic prejudices have a universal impact not only upon its victims but upon everyone. Europe and North America cannot be leaders in democracy if racial inequality is still prevalent. Equality and equity should be the shared interests of every citizen and governments at large.

Conversations about Diversity

We are unable to understand other people's complexity if we do not interact with them and this interaction should go beyond the personal to a wider spectrum such as reading literary materials by those who are part of the narrative, the subjects. It is important to watch and listen to documentaries made by people of colour. Emphasizing the importance of diversity is also paramount. We have to appreciate that diversity is critical as long as inclusion is posited within structures. Conversations on diversity should be obligatory. Not only diversity between different races or cultures but also within the Black community. Black people are not a homogenous community and their experiences are equally variegated. Therefore, it is equally important to talk about the intersecting identities that impinge on their experiences. The experiences of a Black woman may not be the same as those of a Black man.

Acknowledging progress

It is clear that people are more positively predisposed to a positive result and engagement in a success story. Therefore, talking about some of the milestones achieved can definitely work as an antidote to the cynics. It is important to give credit where it is due, highlighting the progress achieved in fighting racism and discrimination both at the societal and institutional level. This is definitely a motivating approach for an audience.

Stranger still: Burdening fellow citizens

Migrants play a central role in the construction of historical narratives in Europe. Migration is as old as humanity; an eternal process where people will continue to move from one place to another on planet earth. We know migration is not something new and it is high time we stopped treating it as though it were a recent phenomenon.

The history of Europe has been marked by departures and arrivals. Having a historical narrative in addition to a political one can help alleviate the 'othering', exclusion and labelling of migrants into a single unit.

The most contentious issue has been whether the cultural diversity prompted by immigrants should be part of European's narrative of diversity. Immigrants and immigration have always been part and parcel of Europe's past, continue to be in the present and shall be the future. In the European diversity narrative, immigrants are not considered to be an integral part of Europe, rather they are seen as single entities whereby the exclusivity of identities is counterfeited and becomes a one dimensional assumption.

This hybridity of a sense of belonging has long been central to diversity. This mixture of identities is on the rise. Individuals are navigating across different forms of belonging that in essence overlap and intersect. Identity therefore has become pluralistic rather than a singular and stark monochrome. The pluralistic nature of identity has redesigned Western societies, leading to their ethnic and cultural diversity which in fact questions the single nation state paradigm.

Sometimes it is like having to choose between a spouse and a lover. You feel like you have to choose one country and its language over something else. The dilemma kicks in, you are torn between two worlds and sometimes the feeling of being in-between resurfaces; the question of either, or. However, having a dual perspective and a double state or sense of belonging can be beneficial at times because one is likely to be in a position to have a broader perspective and world view when not wholly invested in a single identity. There are often however, serious challenges that need to be overcome. Non-immigrants are often reluctant to accept diversity, preferring uniformity; they do not want to see any racks forming. European countries have stalled with their lack of diverse cultural policies that should be instrumental in making Europe a haven for immigration and cultural diversity. Changing political realities are also a hindrance. With Europe's lean towards the Far-right citizenship and identity politics are becoming more volatile than before.

CHAPTER THREE

The Ubiquity of White Supremacy

'Are you ashamed to be Black?' A Polish guy in his mid-30s sitting next to me in a bar once asked me.

The emergence of race in human history was followed by the establishment of a social hierarchy (a racialised social system) that provided well-structured privileges to Europeans (the people who became white) over non-Europeans (the people who became non-white). A racialised system of white supremacy became the global norm and affected all societies where Europeans extended their reach[64].

In the historical context, white supremacy has been widely perceived to be predominant among former colonial masters however, in Europe it is apparent that even countries that never had colonies in Africa or anywhere else are exercising white supremacy; Countries such as Poland, Hungary, Slovakia, and Ukraine among other Central and Eastern European countries.

White power and privilege are fundamentally contingent. The hegemony of whiteness is grounded in structural, historical, and material processes of subjugation, disposition, and imperialism[65].

Whiteness as a Position of status

Whiteness transcends any simple racial categorization; it is indeed a social and institutional status and identity loaded with legal, political, economic and social rights and privileges that are denied to others[66].

The critical race scholar, Cherryl Harris, once conceptualized the advantages that come with white social and economic privileges as "whiteness as property. She explains, 'by according whiteness an actual legal status, an aspect of identity was converted into an external object of property, moving whiteness from privileged identity to a vested interest. The law's construction of whiteness defined and affirmed critical aspects of identity (who is white; of privilege (what benefits accrue to that status; what legal entitlements arise from that status). Whiteness at various times signifies and is deployed as identity, status, and as property, sometimes singularly, sometimes in tandem[67].

Prolific writers such as W.E.B. Du Bois and James Baldwin paid whiteness a lot of attention for many years. They constantly advocated for white people to focus on themselves in search of the implications of being white in a society divaricated by race.

Ruth Frankenberge, a white scholar describes whiteness as multidimensional. These dimensions include a location of structural advantage, a standpoint from which white people look at themselves, at others and at society and a set of cultural practices that are not named or acknowledged[68].

As Bonilla-Silva argues in his book on 'Racism without Racists', while race as a category cannot be abolished, racial structures remain in place for the same reason that other structures do. As members of the dominant race, whites receive material benefits from the racial order, they struggle (or passively receive the manifold wages of whiteness) to maintain their privileges. In contrast, those defined as belonging to the subordinate race or races, struggle to change the status quo (or become resigned to their position). Therein lies the secret of racial structure and racial inequalities in the world order. Bonilla-Silva continues to say that if the goal of the dominant race is to defend its collective interests (i.e., the perpetuation of systemic white privilege) it should surprise no one that this group develops rationalizations to account for the status of the various races.

Reflections on the History of White Supremacy

White supremacy achieved complete ideological and institutional success in the Southern United States between the 1890s and the 1950s and in South Africa between the 1910s and the 1980s, Anti-Semitism in Nazi Germany between 1933 and 1945[69]. Even though these three racist regimes were either deposed or disparaged, the virus of racism and white supremacy cross-fertilized and continues to spread and metastasise into a new malignant shape.

Many people think of white supremacists as those individuals who appear on TV during anti-immigrant demonstrations or that they read about embracing the Nazi salute, attacking Black people, destroying Black people's properties or nationalist Right-wing groups marching and chanting, 'Make Europe pure again' or 'Poland for Poles'. Many white people do not relate to these images of white supremacists and therefore resent this term in its general application.

However, as DiAngelo puts it, the term White supremacist, is used to capture the all-encompassing centrality and assumed superiority of people defined and perceived as white and the practices based on this assumption. Therefore, supremacy does not only apply in the context of individual rationale; it also circumvents the political, economic and social structures of power.

While Bonilla-Silva defines white supremacy as a "racially based political regime and practices that emerged post-fifteenth century that generated ideology to explain and justify racial ordering in society[70], he argues that racism should be conceptualized in structural terms. That is, in what capacities race operates in political, social, economic, and ideological realms to establish, reinforce, and maintain racial hierarchy[71].

Individuals in racialised societies function within social systems where some social actors are racialised as beneficiaries of white supremacy[72]. The race considered superior to others is likely to obtain better economic rewards, entrées to career advancement and better chances in the labor market. It enjoys top status in the political arena and higher social prestige (i.e. is viewed as 'smarter', 'better looking' or non- criminal) and often has license to draw physical (segregation) as well as social (racial etiquette) boundaries between itself and other races. It receives what W.E.B. Dubois called a "psychological wage[73].

We see this a great deal in the employment sector where better jobs and positions are the preserve of White people and in the clandestine employment of African immigrants in various countries across Europe.

Racial Prejudice

People vary in observable physical attributes; there are differences in physical characteristics passed from parents to their offspring either partially or in their entirety. It is the branding of a homogeneous group that characterizes what we now refer to as race. These races are distinct in appearance and to an extent so is their level of development. Some of them may have obtained a good deal on the advanced level of their civilization while others have received a disproportionately small share of advancement.

It is worth noting that the history books indicate that discrimination has existed since time immemorial. 2000 years ago, the ancient Greeks considered themselves different and superior to others, often referring to those who were not Greek as Barbarians (Herodotus). Persians too, regarded themselves as superior to the rest of humanity. There are revelations regarding Aristotle's hypothesis which stated that 'certain people are by nature free from birth and others slaves'. This hypothesis had considerable implications from the 15th century during the enslavement of Black people and Amerindians.[74].

At the onset of African colonization, the discovery of America and of the Transpacific sea route to India, there occurred a fundamental rise in race and color prejudice.

The Darwinian theory of the survival of the fittest was embraced by many white people in support of their policy of expansion and aggression towards those they perceived as being inferior. This theory was widely revered at a time when the European powers were establishing their empires. The theory was instrumental during the colonization period, when colonizers were able to justify their actions. When European rifles were bringing down a part of humanity, they believed they were not just implementing the theory but were trying by any means necessary to replace the inferior with a superior human society. The perception that those who are stronger biologically and scientifically are justified in annihilating the weaker has been widely applied in conflicts within as well as between nations[75].

The truth is that, with colored societies becoming potential competitors in the labor market and claiming the social advantages regarded as exclusively the heritage of the whites, the latter were obviously in need of a pretext for the economic materialism which led them to deny 'inferior' peoples any share in the privileges they themselves enjoyed. For that reason, they warmly welcomed the Darwinian biological thesis. Then by its simplification, distortion and adaptation in order to conform to their own particular interests, it was transformed into so-called 'Social Darwinism' upon which they based their right to social and economic privilege.

The notion of race is so emotionally charged that objective discussion of its significance in relation to social problems is uncommonly difficult. There is no scientific basis whatsoever for a general classification of races according to a scale of relative superiority and racial prejudices and myths are nothing more than a means of finding a scapegoat when the position of individuals and the cohesion of a group is threatened.

It is without doubt that the physical characteristics that have been applied to categorize human races have practical significance to individuals this way endowed. It is also unequivocal that our own civilization puts a premium on physical hue variation in this matter; the darker the skin the less one is considered a normal human being, leading to a constellation of antipathy, demoralization and exclusion. For others, the skin variation becomes so potent that it can create a kind of phobia. These are by no means intrinsic qualities but rather reflect the fabricated untruths and bigotry of the social environment. To uphold the notion that a person is subhuman simply by virtue of having darker skin is absolutely inadmissible. It is like arguing that a black horse will perform more poorly on the track than a white horse. Even though there is little significance in the bigotry connected with skin color, it goes without saying that the mindset and by and large, associated behaviour in most countries goes mainly uncontested.

One of the most irrational aspects of colour prejudice is the categorization of anyone of African heritage as Black regardless of physical appearance. Based on this premise, it is plausible that Black is not a biological term but signifies an affiliation to a specific cultural, economic and social group. In fact, some Black people easily pass for white and are not recognised as Black by many. So, if we could follow the one drop rule that is still prevalent in 21st century where anybody with any African blood is classified as Black, then it would be fair if one drop of white blood makes someone white as well[76].

To demystify the notion that skin colour carries no DNA of inferiority, the repudiated anthropologists; J.H.F Kohlbrugge and doctors such as Reezius, Weinbberg, Segi and Kappers underlined these significant conclusions on race issue;

1. The weight of the frontal lobe, regarded as the seat of intellect, is 44 percent of the total weight of the brain in men and women, Black and white alike.
2. No racial differences are observable as regards the weight of the brain; there are however marked variations between individuals within each human group or race.
3. Men of marked intellectual powers have not necessarily possessed brains greater in weight or volume[77].

Regarding the above findings, we see that there is no connection between inferiority and superiority amongst individuals considered to be from different races.

If we consider the position of Black people and white people, there is the habitual thinking that after so many years, Black people are still inferior to white people. What we forget to acknowledge is that economic, political and cultural advancement lagged because of the historical and current day exploitation that almost every Black person lives today due to colonialism and modern day slavery. Thus far, a Black person is still subjected to neo-colonialism or neo-slavery, if not legal then illegal and by and large, poverty, diseases and demoralization has further contributed to the current situation especially in Africa.

Science, anthropology, evolution and genetics have demystified the myth that any race can be superior to another. It is due to a toxic environment and political and social economics that mean these groups are in their current situation, nothing more than that.

Bigotry

Throughout history, bigotry has prevailed around the world. However, it has not been practised universally, meaning that worldwide, not all people are bigots but its practice has been ubiquitous to the extent that it has managed become a source of conflict among nations and groups within a nation. Bigotry virtually and consistently monopolises discrimination whereby a targeted group of people is oppressed but with the absence of any wrong-doing, thus justifying such oppression. Bigotry has therefore been the foundation of human misery and misapprehension wherever it occurs.

Why are Black people wary of what white people think of them? This matters because to a larger extent, and history can prove this, the life opportunities of Black people especially with regard to careers, depends upon the opinion of White people in power. This validates the common narrative that 'as Black folk, one has to work twice as hard as white folk' to get half as far.

Since race is a social construct with no proven biological foundation as mentioned earlier, it therefore becomes apparent that racial attitudes are derived from existing circumstances and the contacts between others. This is premised on the racial consciousness that is intertwined between society and 'others'. This may be the reason why in some countries, even though people are physically different, they go unnoticed while in others it draws constant attention. In yet others, it paves the way to new laws as was the case in the US with the miscegenation laws that prohibited interracial marriage in some states until 1967. Whilst in other countries, it had no repercussions. The question worth asking is whether race-conflict is due to people having distinctly dissimilar lives or is it about cultural differences in a broader sense.[78]

The Pandemic of Nationalism

POLAND FOR POLES...France for the French...Bulgaria for Bulgarians....

These prevalent slogans are symptomatic of ethnic nationalism coupled with Far-right ideology. This builds on the assumption that there are those who do or do not belong to the national community.

The European Union was founded against the backdrop of historical experience. Europe was once a divided continent that practically destroyed itself during the First and Second World Wars. Spain and Portugal were experiencing Fascism under Fransisco Franco and Antonio Oliveira respectively; Stalin was ruling with an iron fist annexing states in what is now Eastern Europe; and the Nazi regime extended its dominance and occupation to its neighbours Austria, Czechoslovakia and Poland. The idea behind European unification was a singular one, as it moved to form a formidable alliance of states. It was not about conquering or enslaving other countries as they did in 1886 with the Berlin Conference and the Scramble for Africa. Instead of expanding their colonies, Europe expanded its membership through successive accessions. The architects of the European Union wanted to prevent further wars and rooted its alliance in the idea of everlasting peace.

This European project was to create a single economy within a supranational power so that states could think beyond their national borders. The European Union therefore became a post national political organization. However, post-national politics have not been living up to expectations. One of the dilemmas the EU is facing is democracy and the rule of law. The supranational power is found in the European Parliament while states can only vote for national parties. Now the EU is facing another challenge with the re-emergence of nationalism within its own member states. Even though this post-national project has succeeded in creating a single currency and single market, the rise of nationalism and Far-right ideology in its member states has put the union with an equivocal position.

There is a common rhetoric by Far-right parties in Western Europe about immigrants being beneficiaries of social benefits. In fact this mindset is also now prevalent in some Eastern European countries such as Poland where social benefit is extended only to Polish nationals and not immigrants. Many Poles refer to the French experience regarding its stance on immigrants as the backdrop for their assimilation policies. There are some common narratives such as 'you are in Poland, you must speak Polish'; you must adopt Polish culture; if you do not like Poland, then go back to your country; Muslims want to introduce Sharia Law and make Poland a Muslim country.

Far-right groups have used the French experience to further their agenda of not accepting refugees. The French assimilation practise aka *assimilation à la française or action d'assimiler* built upon its colonial policies of assimilation on racial hierarchy and religion is now being over-practised and taken out of the context both by the right and the left in order to forge a collective identity. Debates coalesce particularly around the wearing of the Muslim hijab, something which is not considered to be French.

> *"If you want to become French, you must speak French, you must live like the French and you don't try and change a way of life that has been ours for so many years."...**Nicolas Sarkozy**[79]*

The above words were said by Sarkozy during his Presidential campaign in 2016 calling on immigrants who wish to stay in France to live like 'the French'. Sarkozy's

Nationalism has been a significant political power in transforming the history of Europe and the world for more than 200 years. It has surpassed all notions of freedom, democracy or communism. Due to its transformation, the foundation of modern nationalism was first felt in Western Europe and North America towards the end of the 18th century, before spilling over to other parts of Europe and the rest of the world[80].

Together with socialism, nationalism became one of the two major sets of beliefs of the nineteenth century. In the twentieth century, socialism had unmatched successes and was embraced wholeheartedly across Europe during both the First and Second World War periods in Asia and in Africa. Nationalism could be connected with political, social and economic liberation or with the objective to repress or subjugate others.

Nationalism became the driving-force behind the colonization of Africa and Asia. Between the First and Second World Wars, nationalism became the flag-bearer for oppression. It displaced people from their own countries and rationalized a crusade of territorial invasion.

Nationalism has obviously produced an array of advances whilst becoming a warehouse of perils and prospects, obscuring its own tremendous parallels and incongruity. It could imply liberation and at the very end, tyranny.

The number of nationalist political parties and social movements is increasing at an exponential rate in Europe. As a result of complex issues, Far-right nationalist groups are sweeping across the continent faster than ever. Even though the issues might have some similarities, nationalism varies from country to country depending on the motivation of the Far-right nationalism.

Whether in Rotherham or Rochdale, over 'Muslims' or, about the arrival of Syrian refugees, Far-right groups are often perceived as operating nationally. Research has shown however, that they are not a monolithic entity and that they often create transnational networks. They are manifold, variegated, continuously progressing and often corresponding with one another. They also take advantage of available transnational political networks[81].

Since 2010 in Poland, the Independence March organized on 11th November every year by the Far-right National Radical camp, all Polish Youth and the National Movement has drawn thousands of nationalists from Poland and abroad. These groups focus their anger on bogus external threats such as immigrants and refugees, Islam and Jews as well as internal threats such as the liberal media, Communists and cultural Marxists.

Marches have used slogans such as, 'the whole of Poland sings with us: F*** off with the refugees', 'Not red, not rainbow but national Poland', 'One nation across the borders', and 'F*** Antifa'[82].

Far-right ideologies and practices often permeate national boundaries, making it easier for groups to forge transnational operations. They create new platforms even in the European

Parliament and go as far as making appearances in the street of European cities. There has been a proliferation of engagement of Right-wing groups' in a variety of political issues[83].

*The nationalist Alternative for Germany (AFD) co-chairman Alexander **Alexander Gauland talked of fighting an "invasion of foreigners"** and the party openly focuses on Islam and migration, seeing Islam as something alien to German society. Some of the party's rhetoric has been tinged with Nazi overtones. The AFD sits in the same political family as **France's Far-right National Front** and Austria's Far-right Freedom Party, as well as the populist, anti-Islamic Dutch Freedom Party (PVV) of Geert Wilders. Nigel Farage, former leader of the UK's anti-EU party Ukip, took part in the PVV's 2017 election campaign[84].*

In early March 2020, members of right-wing groups from various European countries were reported to have travelled to Greece to stop migrants from crossing into Greece. According to the groups, this move was a show of solidarity with Greek patriots to defend Europe's borders against immigrants.

A green member of the European Parliament, Erick Marquardt who was on the island of Lesbos at the time, tweeted, 'there are probably 40 international Nazis including convicted criminals here.'[85]

Some anti-fascist and anti-racism civil society groups in Greece have also expressed a profound concern over the presence of a vast group of racists as well as militant neo-Nazis attacking refugees, fuelled by federal and state politics, citing the ongoing mobilization of German neo-Nazis to Greece.[86]

Jobbik, a Hungarian party that was rebranded in 2003, as conservative, anti-communist and anti-globalist has achieved the status of a Far-right party. Jobbik has radical and xenophobic roots and underscoring its position on the refugee crisis of 2015,it profoundly compromised security and the EU's support in working towards a regional solution. Their leaders used inflammatory remarks as Hungary was building walls, declaring states of emergency and deploying soldiers;

> "Hungary has to be able to turn back everyone who arrives at the Hungarian borders as an illegal migrant — everyone without distinction. There is a real humanitarian catastrophe taking place here, but the humanitarian catastrophe is not about what will happen to the poor immigrants. The humanitarian catastrophe is what will happen to poor Hungary."
> −Gabor Vona, Jobbik President, Sept. 2015[87]

In Austria, the identitarian movement, Identitäre Bewegung Osterreichs, was formed in 2012. In 2019, the Austrian government under Chancellor Sebastian Kurz, announced that the government was considering the option of dissolving this right-wing organization, following the revelation that the Christchurch gunman, a 28-year old right-wing extremist from Australia, donated 1500 Euros to the organisation at the beginning of 2018.[88]

The troubling Far Right

Nationalism does not have the same face across Europe

The ubiquity of Far right groups cuts across Europe. These groups target mainly minority groups especially Muslims, Jews, Africans, Roma and the LGBTQ community. Individuals or institutions associated with these groups have also been targeted. In addition, the public discourse on the intolerance faced by migrants and refugees in Europe has been permeated by the checks and balances and collaborations between the Far-right infiltrations and mainstream politics.

Far-right groups have achieved considerable influence in Europe in different capacities such as the political parties in Austria, France and Slovakia triumphing in the 2017 elections.

Modern Europe has been hit by a different form of Far-right that morphs with two main separate stakeholders; Far-right stakeholders have achieved particular influence in both national and European politics. They are constantly attracting new membership, taking their followers to the streets, campaigning to promote their ideas and transnational networks to cross-pollinate their ideologies. The Far-right is also becoming the bedrock of parties and movements that have enjoyed a long existence and have already started to change their representation and political nexus.

The hallmarks of Far-right group insurrections have been multiplying in Europe since 2011.There have also been signs of racist attacks in terms of hate crime, arson, desecration of sacred places and the mushrooming of vigilante groups[89].

One of the most highly publicised Far-right (before the proliferation of the ideology after 2015 migrant crisis)attacks was the mass-shooting of 77 people at a Norwegian Labour Party youth summer camp on Utoya Island, Oslo in 2011 by Aners Behring. During his trial, Behring described his victims as 'traitors who tolerate immigration and encourage the Islamization of Europe.'

Increasingly, it becomes hard to outline Europe's Far-right groups because of their metamorphosis and expanding landscape. Their ideological divisions are coalescing through various interactions such as sport, music and football among others. Many football clubs have now become incorporated into Far- right ideologies.

These clubs include the anti-capitalist, Casa Pound Italia in Italy and the 'Autonomous Nationalists' that was founded in Germany. These two are now bound together both westward and eastward. The most recognizable groups are the white supremacists such as (Blood and Honour, Storm-front), the National Socialists (the most high-profile of which include the National Democratic party of Germany and the party of the Swedes), the pro-identity movements (such as the 'Identitarian Bloc' in France) and the defence leagues (such as the notorious English Defence League). There are also the anti-jihadists such as the new Patriotic Europeans against the Islamization of the Occident (PEGIDA[90]).

The Far-right groups in Europe may have different mandates defining their ideologies but one thing however, is certain. They share a common denominator in criminality. These groups have been found to be engaged in illegal activities such as pimping, extortion, money laundering, drugs and arms, human-trafficking and vigilante activities. There are ongoing criminal trials among the following groups; the National Socialist Underground (Germany), Anti-System Front (Spain), Object 21 (Austria), New Order (Italy), and Roma serial murders and Neo-Nazis who formed their own private militia (Hungary).The year 2015 saw 69 members of the Greek Golden Dawn (XA) (including 18 members of Parliament) vindicated on charges of forming criminal organizations, weapons procurement and soliciting murders[91]. Vigilante groups, taking the law into their own hands, have been at the core of Far-right group mandates.

Right-wing politics have undergone an incredible transformation since the '80s or '90s. Now, they use various mediums, especially social media and even the Church to reach a far wider audience. They use the narrative of migration to lure voters into electing them so as to enter mainstream politics in order to be able to offer up their ideologies to the masses.

In 2019, the New York Times ran a story about how Swedish Far-right websites are being promoted by foreign state and non-state donors. At least six Swedish sites have received financial backing from a Ukrainian/Russian-owned auto-parts business based in Berlin. The distorted view of Sweden pumped out by this disinformation has in turn been used by anti -immigrant parties in Britain, Germany, Italy and elsewhere to stirrup xenophobia and right-leaning voters[92].

In conclusion, it is worth noting the alarming rise of Far-right groups in Europe, not only because of their activities but also as they have not appeared from nowhere. They have their roots in the European Parliament and their respective national parliaments and from local to state institutions. They mature very well in an environment where state institutions fail. Fascism does not exist in a vacuum. It survives and evolves in an environment of authoritarian structures, hibernating within the cocoon of law-enforcement and law-makers.

The 2017 Presidential elections in Austria and Slovakia were a litmus test that ushered in the nationalistic rhetoric now permeating mainstream politics. The two major parties in both Slovakia and Austria paid attention to the anti- immigrant rhetoric that was fuelled by Far-right groups and subsequently shifted to the right. Another distorted political order is that of the right-wing government in Poland, which began infringing on fundamental freedoms as soon as it came to power in 2015, totally shifting the country's political dialogue towards the right. Freedoms such as freedom of the press, women rights to abortion and the independence of constitutional courts have been compromised.

The refugee crisis and terrorist-attacks across Europe have created a breeding ground for Far-right groups to promote their anti-immigrant and anti-Muslim ideologies and to sell them to the general public. In fact right-wing groups have gained a lot of support because of their anti-immigrant and anti-Muslim stance.

It is a fact that the recent elections across Europe projected an exponential gain for Far-right parties that campaigned with openly xenophobic rhetoric. The triumph in March 2016 for the Alternative for Germany (AFD) in the German regional elections and two Far-right parties, Slovak National Party (SNS) and the People's Party Our Slovakia (L'SNS) in the Slovak national elections are cases in question. Moreover, opinion polls in countries such as France, Austria and the Netherlands show equal promise for Populist Radical Right (PRR) parties. Though not all European countries have witnessed the successful mobilization of the PRR, it is fair to conclude that this section is fairing very well[93]. However, it would be incorrect to conclude that PRR parties have flourished only under the banner of migration concerns

Immigration obviously absorbs the central concerns of PRR parties. Even though there were anti-immigration issues voiced during the election period, the recent European refugee crisis became a central part of immigration discourse in Central and Eastern European countries. The immigration issue has become even more of a concern in post-Communist states. This can be seen readily in the rhetoric of political party leader kingpins such as Jaroslaw Kaczynski of Poland, Hungarian Prime Minister, Victor Orban and Robert Fico of Slovakia.

This can be seen to translate to a public opposition to multiculturalism as illustrated by the position these parties take on cultural matters. Most scholars have suggested that these parties embrace national culture as a primary concern.

Socioeconomic matters become a secondary concern to PRR parties' manifestos[94].

Table 1: Far right parties across Europe

Country		Party	Description
Italy	Matteo Salvini	leader of the League	Nationalist Spearheaded anti-immigration policy Euro-sceptic vision
Germany		Alternative for Germany (AfD)	Anti-euro party. Pushed for strict anti- immigration policies. Embraces hostility towards Islam. Stronghold in Eastern Germany. Threatens to deport all immigrants.
Spain		Vox party	Embraces the unity of the Spanish state.
Austria	Sebastian Kurz	Peoples Party Freedom Party(FPÖ)	Anti- immigrant policies
France	Marine le Pen	National Front(FN)/ National Rally(Rassemblement National)	Anti- immigration Anti-euro Anti-Semitic
Sweden		Sweden Democrats (SD)[1]	Neo-Nazi roots Anti—immigration
Finland		Finns Party	Anti immigration Anti-climate change policies
Estonia		Conservative People's	Anti- immigration

Country	Leader	Party	Position
		Party of Estonia (EKRE)	Same sex marriage
Poland	Jaroslaw Kaczynski	conservative Law and Justice (PiS) Confederation party	Strong on nationalism, social welfare and Catholic church.
Hungary	Viktor Orban	Fidesz Party Jobbik	Defender of Hungary and Europe against Muslim migrants
Slovenia		Slovenian Democratic Party(SDS)	Supporter of Urban
Greece		Greek Solution Golden Dawn	Anti- immigrants

SOURCE: BBC.COM[95]

White Privilege

LOOKING AT WHITE PRIVILEGE from the standpoint of someone who is not part of it sets a tone towards understanding the racial inequalities prevalent in our modern societies. To understand the adverse ramifications of white privilege, it is essential to grasp its impact on those who do not benefit from it.

1. https://www.bbc.co.uk/news/world-europe-45466174

The word 'privilege' makes many white people uncomfortable. The reality is that, if one is born White whether in Europe, Africa or America, that person is born privileged. Many people may not feel comfortable with this statement; unfortunately this is what it is. People talk about racism but there are allegedly no racists, about homophobia whilst there are no homophobes, about Islamophobia but no Islamophobes and misogyny is talked about whilst there are no misogynists. And then there is Afrophobia, with no one acknowledging they are Afrophobe.

White skin privilege does not guarantee a perfect life nor does it imply that one comes from an affluent background. White privilege is not an automatic mandate for prosperity. It simply implies that one is more advantaged than those who are non-white.

White privilege means that you were born with an intrinsic advantage over any other race, white skin being a guarantor for bypassing many obstacles. It comes with many benefits that are not shared by non-whites. White privilege is a contentious topic and its discussion is often met with resistance and defensiveness. Trying to explain white privilege to a beneficiary is bound to elicit strong opposition. White privilege offers white people incentives and opportunities that are not enjoyed by non-whites particularly Black people. It gives white people increased leverage over a whole spectrum of life, rendering them impervious to a set of challenges that non-whites have to face.

Finally, White privilege remodels the world we live in and how we connect with each other and the rest of the world.

The Incentives of White privilege

The quintessential nature of white privilege is that it gives white people an advantage over many of life's realities. There are myriad life hazards that White people do not have to confront, tackle or even notice. For instance; their skin colour does not affect people's perception of how they dress their job performance and other social and economic responsibilities.

White people have immunity from random police searches and do not experience police harassment due to their 'perceived' race. White people do not have to tell their children how to behave when they are pulled over by the police. White people are equally not afraid when they are pulled over by police, are not followed around shops by security guards or suspected of stealing merchandize because of their colour.

White skin privilege shields them from the reality of the experiences that Black people face; that Black people are typically thought to represent a hard-edged masculinity, long suffering and oppressed, not very well educated, sexually prolific, smoke weed and are a father to many.

White skin privilege does not enslave White people to another person's idea of what it is to be white.

I believe most White people are little concerned with any of the above issues. They enjoy these privileges because there are institutions created by whites that reinforce racism, discrimination and xenophobia.

The incentives and leverage that white skin privilege enjoys considerably remodels the way the world views other races.

Any discussion on civilization also puts white people above the rest. White people are the civilized ones, while the rest are followers and should conform to their civilization. This dystopian view of Africa is being shared by even non-whites with Africa for many years being considered a dark continent, savage, wild and uncivilized.

A look at school curricula in most European countries shows textbooks full of praise for White people as the sole contributor to the world's advancement. Black people are just footnotes and in many places, their history is erased entirely. And when African history surfaces, it always starts with post-independent Africa.

White people also control the media and use it to reinforce stereotypes about the African continent. Rarely is anything positive reported in the Western media about Africa. This makes it difficult to appreciate the continent's magnificent flora and fauna, its rich cultural traditions and thriving modern cities for example. Media portrayals of the continent are marred by negativities. White people are widely represented in public spaces while Black people are kept out of the foreground; take for example monuments. It is not a common sight to see monuments to Black people in European cities even though they contributed widely to Europe's advancement.

A recent case in Denmark which gained world attention was when two artists of African Descent erected a 23 feet tall statue of a Black woman in Copenhagen[96]. Her head is wrapped and she stares straight ahead whilst sitting barefoot, in a wide-backed chair , clutching a torch in one hand and a tool used to cut sugar cane in the other.[97]. The statue was widely criticized by white people who did not understand its significance.

Entitlement: Part of Structural White Society

Lukwesa Burak ✓
@LukwesaBurak

My heart cracked... #ClimateCrisis #ClimateChange
@GretaThunberg twitter.com/vanessa_vash/s...

Vanessa Nakate @vanessa_vash
Share if you can
What it means to be removed from a photo!
twitter.com/i/broadcasts/1...

♡ 60   7:10 PM - Jan 24, 2020

💬 36 people are talking about this

SOURCE: BBC.COM[98]

VANESSA NAKATE WAS not a household name to many people, until her story was featured in mainstream international media. Vanessa, a young Ugandan climate activist, surfaced during the Davos conference. Being the only Black activist among her white peers, her photo was cropped out from a group photo which was taken with prominent activists including Greta Thunberg, Loukina Tille, Luisa

Neubauer and Isabelle Axelsson, after a news conference. Ms. Nakate said that numerous outlets, including the American AP news agency removed her from the photos[99]. She expressed her dismay in one of her Twitter posts:

"We don't deserve this. Africa is the least emitter of carbon, but we are the most affected by the climate crisis.You erasing our voices won't change anything. You erasing our stories won't change anything," she said.

"I don't feel ok right now. The world is so cruel."[100]

Peers such as Greta Thunberg came to her defence calling the incident out for its racism and unacceptability. Vanessa's case is representative of the silencing of Black voices where White people feel entitled to represent us and take credit for it. Her case is just a microcosm of the prevalent but subtle entitlement where Black voices are silenced for White people's self-righteousness and ownership.

Entitlement also works as the backdrop of toxic white nationalism, where non-whites are blamed and condemned for their personal predicaments and problems, especially economic ones. They feel their circumstances should be better because they are white, shunning those who are not for taking away the possibility of the good life from them. They believe non-whites are entering their countries to benefit from their wealth when frankly, this perceived wealth was created by the blood and sweat of Black people.

Whiteness gives access to good education, employment, services etc at the expense of 'others'. These are the facts of white life. Even though the transformative nature of white entitlement has changed from de jure to de facto, its lack of acknowledgement becomes a problem.

The silencing of Black voices where White people feel entitled to represent us (Black),and take credit for it, is fundamental in understanding how privilege and entitlement operates. The prevalent but subtle entitlement where Black voices are silenced for White people's self-righteousness and ownership is worthy of discourse. This is the entitlement to occupy a space not just meant for you, the entitlement to not see or recognize the work of Black people.

White Fragility

I have Black friends; my best friend is from Zimbabwe, I cannot be racist........

You do not have a right to be judgmental of me because you do not know me.....

You know, I am a good person therefore I cannot be racist. It is your own opinion and it does not show who I am.......

Black people always play the race card even when there is no racism in order to make white people feel guilty......

THIS IS THE CONTINUUM of defense mechanisms that many white people resort to when approached by Black people on the subject of racism. One can almost smell the discomfort and defensiveness emerging when they are challenged.

Even though discriminatory and racist practices have been prevalent and obvious, many people still characterize racism as a problem of skinheads or Nazi apologists. Some also believe that once they are cognizant of historical racist practices such as slavery, they are not racist. Their reaction exposes the inherent essence of white fragility that hinders efforts to respond and prevent racism. Most people feel that their values and principles are avowedly unracist and therefore they are not part of the discussion, never mind the problem. Even though the intensity of their practices may vary and not manifest themselves in the way of skinheads, it is equally pernicious and debilitating to contend with. These are the circumstances where the more opaque patterns of racism should be exposed and deliberated upon.

The term 'White fragility' was coined by race scholar Robin DiAngelo in 2011 to project the lack of interest by White people when their opinions on race and racism are contested, especially when they are drawn into discussions of white supremacy. Black people who openly talk about racism are often considered offensive and racist. This is one of the reasons most Black people do not engage in white fragility discourse because of the social cost that they risk. They often therefore keep quiet in order to keep the peace, protect their businesses, their status and in some cases, their families.

White fragility holds racism to ransom. We all see colours and it would be disingenuous to suggest that some people are colour blind to race or racism, especially when we are living in a divided and polarised society. The adherence to a position of racial innocence by white people is a mandate for ubiquitous racism and discrimination. It more or less serves their personal interest and complicity. It projects a parochial attitude that prejudice will disappear once we stop talking about it. Racism will not disappear just because people refrain or recoil from the discourse. The more that people choose to ignore issues of race, the more society becomes viscerally divided and unequal; in short, it becomes a minefield.

> "I have a racist worldview. I have developed racist patterns. I have investments in this system of racism because it has served me well."The racist status quo is comfortable for me virtually 24/7. ...**DiAngelo**"[101]

These were statements meant to provoke an audience to engage in the white fragility discourse and to expose the uneasiness that white people feel once their racial tendencies are revealed. In her book 'White Fragility' she explains that white people obstruct discussions of race, power and racial hierarchy because of the feeling of anger and a refusal to engage.

On several occasions both verbally, via email and on social media, I have been told that it is pointless to continue to talk about racism because nothing is going to change. That if I don't like the country I live in or if I don't like Europe, I should go back to Africa. I believe that these kind of narratives are directed at many Black people who have dared to try to expose white fragility. I also believe that most if not all of the above claims would relate to every white person reading them.

White people are also presumptuous when it comes to acknowledging racism. More often than not they will argue that racism is just ignorance and unconscious bias and since they are not biased, they cannot be racist. Another assumption is that a white person cannot be racist when they have Black friends. It is as if having one or two black friends shields one from becoming a racist. In fact some 'friends of Black' are equally bad as 'enemies of Black'.

Some would also argue that there are more serious problems in the world and Black people should move on because racism is not an important issue as other world problems.

Functions of White

The reason why racism is hard to eradicate is the fact that many white people both at the societal and institutional level are reluctant to acknowledge its morbid existence. The worst racist is one that turns a blind eye towards this heinous act for they perpetuate and reinforce racism, condoning at both the societal and institutional level. If only they were be cognizant of the connection between historical and contemporary racism rather than silencing any efforts made towards its elimination. They would shift the focus from the messenger to the message and proactively engage Black people in the discourse on race matters without any malevolence. This behaviour blocks any entry point for reflection and engagement. Furthermore, they block the ability to repair racial fissures and exacerbate the chasm between different races.

It is obvious that Europe has a race problem. There is a profound uneasiness in race classification. The discourse that 'we are a human race' is predominant and often forms the backdrop of White fragility. Of course we are undeniably a human race, however, failing to recognize the social construct of race totally hinders the efforts to address the manifestations of pronounced racism and the prominent racial divide.

It is human nature that sometimes we become passive about things that matter and have outbursts about things that do not, In fact everything matters; it depends on what trajectory you are looking at. It is without a doubt that many white people are reluctant to talk about race and at the very least tend to think that race has no place in modern society. Some would argue that they are not responsible for creating or modelling the term race, thereby devaluing the currency of race discourse. I have heard on numerous occasions white folks refraining from talking about racism and regularly reiterate the banality of diversity; that globalized society is multicultural and that racism has no place in it. In other words, their disdain towards a discourse on racism begins with their lack of acknowledgement of the problem.

Expats vs. immigrants: A hierarchy of titles

Africans are immigrants, Asians are immigrants, Arabs.... are immigrants. However, Europeans are expats because they are superior to the rest. Immigrant is a term reserved for 'inferior races'.

WE KNOW THAT MIGRATION is as old as humanity and has existed in different forms with various pull and push factors whether internally or across borders. However, migration comes with a varied lexicon based on myths and biases ingrained within race discourse and thus circumventing white supremacist ideology.

In reality, any person leaving his or her country for employment purposes abroad is an expatriate regardless of the colour of their skin or geographical location. However, this reality only applies to white people. The lexicon of migration is marred by a racial hierarchy by which white people are placed at the top, above everyone else. Any white person going to work abroad whether in Africa or any other place should be an immigrant unless the individual fits the specific categorization of an expatriate devoid of any racial affiliation.

The discourse on the lexicon of migration is something that is very visible in the media, civil society and human rights organisations. The hierarchy of categories in the movement of people from their home countries into their host countries has been marred by different terminologies such as expats, migrants, immigrants, asylum seekers and refugees among others. What constitutes these categorizations? What is the origin of these kinds of categorizations? And why are these images created in order to define one to be any of them? Without contextualizing these terminologies, the dictionary definitions shed some light as to their variations.

Wikipedia provides a more detailed definition of these terminologies; an expatriate (shortened to expat) is a person residing in a country other than their native country. The term often refers to professionals, skilled workers or artists taking positions outside their home country, either independently or sent abroad by their employers, which are usually private companies, universities, governments or nongovernmental organizations. Effectively, migrant workers, they usually earn more than they would at home, and less than the local employees. However, the term expatriates is also used to refer to retirees and others who have chosen to live outside their native country[102]. Historically, it has also referred to exiles. However, it does not categorically explain their earning power both in their native and host countries, unlike the case of migrants who earn more than they would in their home countries.

According to the Cambridge Dictionary, an expatriate is someone who does not live in their own country. Going by this definition, probably many people think of expats as those white people sitting by the pool sipping expensive gin and tonics, living in expensive houses or something of that nature. The reality of this image lurks within the social hierarchy.

According to the United Nations, an international migrant is someone who changes his or her country of usual residence, irrespective of the reason for migration or legal status. The term migrant refers to someone moving from one country to another legally.

From the above definitions, we can see that there is no connection to the difference in skin colour, ethnicity or country of origin. Therefore, in everyday usage, we would expect these terminologies to be applied equitably. However, this is far from the reality. When we apply these terminologies in context, the differences rapidly become apparent. In European public dicourse, these terminologies are grouped into two categories; those for expats and those for immigrants, where expats are a group of white western people working abroad while immigrants are the rest, even if they are just as skilled workers or diplomats going back to their native countries upon completion of their tenure.

The origins of expatriates is related to the colonial period in Africa, India and America. Europeans moving to their respective colonies to establish businesses were often referred to as expats. They were often sent with attractive packages such as free housing, and free education for their children. They were automatically called expats by locals and governments to distinguish them from the local population. There was a great disparity between the two whereby expats often had more rights and protection than locals.[103]

The Guardian published an article in 2015 entitled, 'Why are white people expats when the rest of us are immigrants' by Mawuna Remarque Koutonin arguing that the word 'expat' is a label 'reserved exclusively for Western white people going to work abroad. According to Koutonin, the word 'immigrant' is set aside for everyone else i.e. those considered to be part of an inferior race[104].

Five years later, the connotations of this term have barely changed. These titles are often used to discriminate others. Since the 2015 refugee crisis, the term immigrants and migrants has been widely used interchangeably to refer to people crossing the Mediterranean to Europe. Whilst expat has been connected with a class, a term that seems more befitting than 'immigrant', even when they settling in their host country permanently.

The Corpus of Global Web-Based English (GloWbE), conducted research on the usage of these terminologies relating to expats and immigrants. In the table below, the words featured at the top denote the strongest frequency in relation to either immigrants or expats[105].

According to studies published on *linguisticpulse.com,* the two words contain the following multiplicity of connotations;

———————————
———————————

Top 20 adjectives occurring near EXPAT and IMMIGRANT in internet language

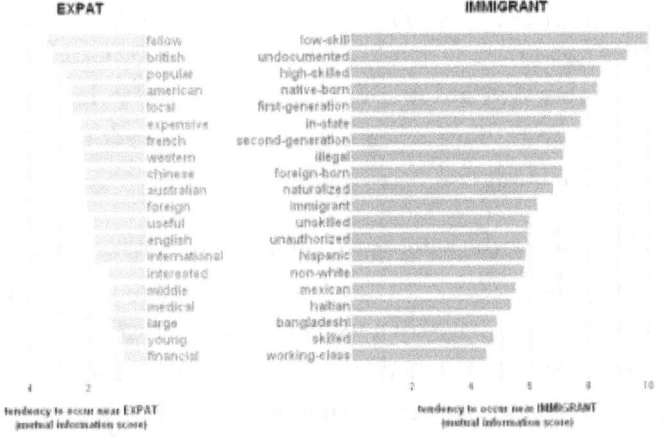

EXPAT

fellow
british
popular
american
local
expensive
french
western
chinese
australian
foreign
useful
english
international
interested
middle
medical
large
young
financial

IMMIGRANT

low-skill
undocumented
high-skilled
native-born
first-generation
in-state
second-generation
illegal
foreign-born
naturalized
immigrant
unskilled
unauthorized
hispanic
non-white
mexican
haitian
bangladeshi
skilled
working-class

tendency to occur near EXPAT
(mutual information score)

tendency to occur near IMMIGRANT
(mutual information score)

linguisticpulse.com

THE COMMON NARRATIVE of why white people are expats while the rest of us are immigrants should not be taken for granted within the context of race discourse. One of the reasons why white people refer to themselves as expats is due to the notion that they are better placed and above others. The superiority rationale which at some point is fuelled by the historical subjugation of other races was actually premised during era of slavery and colonization.

It is apparent that modern Europe is becoming more racially charged when it comes to the lexicon of migration. I have seen and read about Polish right-wing groups demonstrating in the UK, holding banners with 'immigrants go home'. It shows that they actually do not understand this lexicon of migration, believing that only non-white people can be immigrants. The idea that underlies this is that white people believe Black people to be less intelligent and are just menial workers running away from harsh conditions in their countries. The reality is that Africans or Black people moving to Europe or those who were born in Europe are not monolithic in the nature of their migration process.

Neo-Nazi and right-wing parties have also been instrumental in shaping the discourse on migrants in Europe. Across Europe, right wing parties have been using the 2015 refugee (migrant) crisis to further their agenda in the media. The media has also been at the forefront of exploiting the usage of this word. The media has for example, created the false impression that all migrants are illegal. Even though they know the difference between migrants, asylum seekers and refugees, they usually band together everyone moving to Europe from any developing country as a refugee. The media has also been strident in spreading the propaganda of an invasion of Europe by illegal migrants. The main right-wing parties in Europe such as German AFD, Lega in Italy, and RN in France and the FPO in Austria have taken a leading role in alarming their people about this inversion[106].

According to Eurostat, the number of people residing in an EU Member State with citizenship of a non-member country on 1 January 2018 was 22.3 million, representing 4.4 % of the EU-28 population. Meanwhile, there were 17.6 million people living in one of the EU Member States on 1 January 2018 with citizenship of another EU Member State[107]. Therefore, the rhetoric of an invasion of Europe by immigrants is pure propaganda designed to stoke the fears of EU citizens and limit immigrant numbers.

─────────────

Travelling while Black

TRAVELLING IS A FASCINATING phenomenon for many people. You get to see parts of the world that you never knew and to meet people you never imagined meeting; (some can be idiots, just like anywhere else). Travelling in Europe comes with a lot of surprises. There is of course the chance of meeting xenophobes at the same time as very nice people, friendly and open to foreigners and tourists.

Europe is so diverse that every country is different in its own way and the traditions, culture as well as people are different too. Experiences therefore are varied even within the same country.

People of African Descent are spread all over Europe from small villages to big cities, with multitude experiences. In some countries, the sight of a Black person in a small village definitely arouses a lot of curiosity.

Travelling between cities you notice little difference due to multiculturalism, however visiting places outside the main cities can arouse a great deal of interest though also apathy. Some places can be traditional where people are hospitable and some places are more family oriented. A visit to a village can turn out to be a whole village event. Some places may also be dangerous for a person of colour, where one may experience racist abuse such as 'go back to Africa' or 'you are not welcome here'. Being careful as a precaution should suffice.

While most countries in Europe have been exposed to a taste of African culture and her people, through artistry, cuisine or literature, there is still a laziness of mindset towards People of African Descent. Some countries, especially in Eastern Europe have little experience with Africans and the sudden appearance of African migrants often represents a big challenge for them. These encounters can come with a great deal of prejudice.

Having travelled to some places where the locals have never seen a single Black face, it became obvious to me that ignorance and prejudice are deeply embedded in the minds of some white people. Physical features squarely put one at the centre of curiosity among locals. On my travels I saw people elbowing each other, pointing sharply towards me and staring.

I have known people to follow me at close quarters or find their way into a shop just to get a better look at me. There were situations when a person would start a random conversation in English just to practise or show their friends that they knew the language. My response has always been to say a few words in the local language. It is at moments like these that the already exotic status of a black person becomes even more pronounced.

On many occasions I have been asked to pose for photos with strangers and sometimes I have caught people stealthily taking pictures of me without my consent. I have been to places especially in Poland, where some people compare their skin colour to mine. When I had dreadlocks, people were often keen to touch them; becoming so annoying when people would just touch them whenever they felt like it and talked about it as they were always curious about its texture.

There are a lot of interactions and engagements in the world and obviously if the local people have never seen a Black person before, there will be a curiosity and that will definitely find a way of being addressed. Engaging with them, however hard it might be sometimes, could be the best message to send people.

As a Black man who travels frequently and extensively, I am shocked by the role and proliferation of overt prejudice in relation to Black people. For many Black people, travelling abroad has not been a positive experience whilst to some it presents the possibilities of open-mindedness and looking at the world through a different prism.

I once encountered a ridiculous situation at airports in Poland and Montenegro whilst checking in and out respectively. The Polish example was the most outrageous as it involved the least expected individual. After checking through passport control, I went straight through to the gate where personnel proceeded to spend considerable time verifying my Polish residency card. Many of these incidents occur whilst I am travelling to attend human rights conferences, training or workshops and in most of the cases I travel as part of a group. Nonetheless, on this occasion, it led to the intervention of an immigration officer. Clearly this kind of situation should not arise; for one, they had to authenticate a residency card and secondly, they were not verifying the passport of other passengers who were white. It was a pure case of racial profiling based on skin colour.

The other example was when I was going through security check Podgorica airport in Montenegro. After passing through the metal detector, (following a colleague who was also Black), the security guy swapped the screening for a drug test. This is bearing in mind that one of our white colleagues had been in front of us and another one behind. Needless to say, they had not been tested for drugs. When I confronted the security lady, as always, she believed she knew how to defend such a racist move. She said exactly what I had expected her to say. That it was 'standard procedure' and that the procedure was done randomly, because they always locate quotas and we fell within the prescribed quota.

I found this preposterous, by definition; for we did not fall within 'random sampling' due to the way we were sorted out. We had a heated argument and made sure that they understood the consequences of their actions. This kind of experience is not something new; many Black people regularly report similar experiences at airports, train stations or crossing borders. Personnel always have a justification for their racist acts.

From my own experience and from the stories I have heard from other Black people, what follows are some of the most commonly reported experiences. I must emphasize that there may be some Black people who never or only partially experience such things. This does not mean that they are not happening. All these things I outlined below are real. Personally, I have experienced all of them.

The exotic status: This involves responding to obnoxious questions about your looks; skin colour and hair texture and being met always head on with prejudices about the Black community. This is a form of alienation, akin to feeling like a stranger in a society where one is actually integrated.

The 'nod'. Even though this is a Black gesture, it often arouses curiosity from white people. I've been asked many times by white people why Black people always nod or greet others who they barely know. My response is, it is just a Black thing. I often find myself nodding automatically to fellow Black strangers almost as a reflex that we have been conditioned into as a way of saying, yeah, this is family. It is a kind of acknowledgement and recognition that sometimes leaves those around perplexed.

Being an Ambassador for the Black Community and Africa: Often you are ascribed de facto expert status on African affairs. Any tragedy in Africa will require your attentive response. Your actions will be representative and in most cases you will try to act correctly in order not to tarnish the image of the Black community. Expect to be asked if you know a friend from Nigeria or Zimbabwe, as if you are expected to know all Africans in that country. You will be constantly reminded that there is one African guy you resemble; some will call you John as if every Black man is John. It also means that you may be subjected to some very unintelligent questions such as how is Africa, as if Africa is a country. Other questions such as do you live with animals or what means of transport do you use in Africa. As if every Black person has come directly from Africa.

White Saviour

UNQUALIFIED MISSIONARY denies she sought to portray herself as a doctor at centre where at least 105 children died... **The Guardian**[108]

Renee Bach, a Missionary 'Playing Doctor' for Years in Uganda, Sued for Causing the Deaths of At Least Two Babies... Atlanta Blackstar[109]

*Renee Bach wasn't a doctor, but she still treated many patients in Uganda, lawsuit says....***ABC news**[110]

Renée Bach went to Uganda to save children—but many in her care died. Was she responsible?...The New Yorker[111]

Naive volunteers, teenagers with no experience and not even a college education are deluded into believing that their destiny is to make a big difference 'working' in Africa. They often fundraise for their trip across the globe, soliciting funds from organizations, family, and friends and sometimes their church in order to embark upon a journey that is actually not indispensable in the least.

They go to Africa, start non-governmental organizations, even sometimes adopting children. Even though their intentions may be perceived to be genuine and well-intentioned this is never validated when seen within the context of what is known as white saviour complex; 'we are the ones who can save those poor Africans'.

The intentions of the white saviour are often revered by recipients who are oblivious of the motive behind it; the self-fulfilment, self-gratification and sense of gaining from the misery of others. That is, until things take a wrong turn.

This was the case of Renee Bach, a 19-year old white American woman who went to Uganda in 2009 and founded an NGO to help malnourished children. In an interview with New Yorker magazine, she reiterated that *'she had felt called to Africa to help the needy, and she believed that it was Jesus' will for her to treat malnourished children'*[112]. It is alleged that at least 105 children later died under her care. Renee did not have any medical training and the facility from which she operated was not a health clinic, but actually her own home.

In one of her blogs, which was later used as evidence in a lawsuit, she describes her work in 2011. *"I hooked the baby up to oxygen and got to work..I took her temperature, started an IV, checked her blood sugar, tested for malaria, and looked at her HB count"*. Other witnesses mentioned that she used to dress in a clinical coat, often had a stethoscope around her neck. A disturbing account was given by a Ugandan driver who stated that on average, he would drive at least seven to ten bodies of children back to their villages each week[113].

'White saviour' is a term that warrants considerable scrutiny due to the potential implications for those at the receiving end. Reaching out to someone in need shows us how much we appreciate humanity and are ready to help those in dire need. Africa is a continent with a great number of problems be it financial, civil unrest, famine, poverty or disease. There is a great deal that needs to be done to alleviate these problems.

The United Nations has outlined its Sustainable Development Goals (SDGs), a successor of Millennium Development Goals (MDG), with structures for every member state to initiate and implement. National governments too have their own budget and programs to tackle the most problematic areas. However, no government can meet all the requirements for various reasons one of which is of course, corruption. This exists in other parts of the world though to a different magnitude. Poor economic growth has displaced many Africans and prompted their movement within and outside the continent. This is where humanitarian and development NGOs, institutions, philanthropists and benevolent individuals fill the gap. They attempt to deliver services that national governments have failed to provide.

This seemingly benevolent instinct has always been historically entangled in race issues and white supremacy, sometimes in a blatant manner and other times in the name of volunteerism and voluntourism etc. Many Africans are outspoken about how Western NGOs have used their resources- in some cases an enormous amount of funding to initiate self-serving projects in some African countries which turn out to be but a projection of their own interests. Voluntourism has been one of the more recent, fashionable phenomena, whereby Western organizations or individuals organize a trip to African slums, take photos of destitute children and post them on social media.

In this way they are directly benefitting from others' misery. Whilst some do have an ulterior motive, others see it as an opportunity to do something good and to consolidate funds for sustainable projects. Nevertheless, the most controversial issue is the white saviour tendencies exhibited by most people involved in these projects; as exhibited in social, educational or governmental policies or just movies or documentaries, the white saviour or messiah complex shares many of the elements of white supremacy.

Four ways Europeans are Taught to be White saviours

1. Celebrity philanthropy

SOME CELEBRITIES PERFORM real- life hero roles as philanthropists and find a variety of social causes to endorse in the so called, developing world.

I believe most of us have seen the white messiah or white savoir roles in films especially in Hollywood movies; the generous and kind-hearted white person going to poor countries to help locals overcome their predicament. I'm referring to movies such as Cry Freedom or Django. They depict white people as the savoir of the desperate poor who have been waiting for a white person to appear and save them. The white messiah complex is a belief that 'we have all the answers and it is our responsibility to save these people'.

Media representation plays an essential role in influencing people's perceptions of how they view the world.-Hollywood has equally played a huge role in shaping the way we see the world. Take for instance, the movie *The Blind Side: Evolution of a Game* based on Michael Lewis' book that gives an in-depth account of the success of a Black athlete. In the movie, with Sandra Bullock as its heroine, her white family is portrayed as taking care of the Black kid and becomes responsible for his success.

There are actually many movies of this kind. They focus on the true story of a family, for example, the Tuoys, who rescued Michael Oher, a Black teenager from a very poor background and who went on to become an NFL player. This movie depicts white people as racially compassionate actors. The racial narratives in the movie reinforce the stereotypes and prejudices of Black people; drug use, baby mama, arrogance, gangs and crime-infested neighborhoods. The film sanctifies the benevolence of a white person and shows that the only way Oher could be saved is through this white compassion. To the rest of the world, this film sends certain messages, reinforcing the apparently central tenets, that;

White people are the saviours.

Black people can only prevail with the help of white people.

Black neighborhoods are essentially precarious.

Black people are poor, promiscuous and often drug addicts..

The only way Black people can excel is through sport.

Hollywood movies are one of the main instruments for establishing this sort of apartheid mindset. Even though they might use the characters as a drama, what happens is that they are essentially reinforcing and perpetuating the message of white supremacy. Through the process of controlling and manipulating the images of Black people and policing their bodies, Black people became the on-looked, not the lookers. White people therefore become the controllers of what is to be seen and how it is seen.

2. School

A Colonial perspective

Schools in Europe are predominantly white, with their Eurocentric curriculum that promotes the narrative that Western civilization is better than the rest. With there being so little about Africa, many Europeans believe that their civilization is by far the superior. There is the narrative that Western civilization has achieved what other civilizations have never managed and that in some crucial way, other civilizations have not contributed to the modern world.

This means that Europeans develop a superiority complex (that they are better than any other civilization). Education has certainly played a central role in over-overcompensating European accomplishments in the world. When our upbringing is defined by how successful and how much better we are than others, we develop a superiority complex that only we are able to solve the world's problems and that our whiteness is superior.

In age of the internet, there is much information that people can access to enlighten and re-educate. We can learn and understand that other civilizations also contributed enormously to the modern world. Miseducation has been one of the pillars of white savior complex.

1. Foreign policy

The West is very active when it comes to rescue-packages for troubled African countries. In the event of natural calamities, we are habituated to seeing images of Western countries pouring in humanitarian aid to assist affected countries. This phenomenon is also instrumental in advancing foreign policy. Therefore the West is often celebrated as the mighty, brave and heroic in leveraging their foreign policy to intervene in the bad fortunes of oppressed states. On the flipside, their intervention is often questionable as to whether it is doing more harm than good, such as the case of Libya.

In many ways the West does not seem to have even a minimal grasp of the complexity of the problems they are trying to fix in Africa. In contrast to those who are directly affected, the West cannot solve the problems relating to these calamities. Africa has experienced a long history of misplaced foreign-imposed policies that have not worked in the long-term. For example, the IMF's "structural adjustment programs" which failed dismally; the militarization of countries such as Somalia, DRC, the presence of AFCON, some short-lived, agricultural policies and commodity exploitation in some poor African countries; the support of corrupt governments and French-Afrique- the French influence in Francophone countries. These are just some of the structures for maintaining power in Europe's former colonies.

Foreign aid, which is a regular feature of the discourse on helping Africa, has exposed the West as being short-sighted and indifferent to the complexity of the problems the continent is facing. The West has divested its largesse in the form of aid, money which often ends up in the wrong hands. Western donors often assume they have the best solution to every problem in the continent. In fact, some of the West's foreign policies promote conditions that actively create opportunities for white savior volunteerism.

Volunteerism as a Form of Commercialisation: When Diligence becomes a non-priority

Travelling volunteers have for a long time made volunteering a self-fulfilling initiative, with little acknowledgement of the real consequences of their activities. For many Westerners, volunteering in Africa has been more of an emotional experience with traces of white privilege. It satisfies their appetite for wanting to 'do something good', for that the feeling of doing something worthy is of course, emotionally enriching. It therefore becomes unnecessary to ask if what they are doing is actually benefiting those in need. It is equally important to realize that lending a helping hand to the needy abroad should not be a means of presenting ourselves as heroes but a means of helping the needy to help themselves.

My point is that, helping is a human instinct and we need to help those in need as it is the most honorable thing one can do. However, there is a need to reflect upon and assess the context of one's volunteering. Helping those who are destitute for self-fulfilment and gratification is a stark contradiction of purported intent. Very often you see these people flaunting their Facebook profiles with photos of them surrounded by local children indeed, a trip to Africa is never complete without a group photo or selfie with local children. It seems as though the volunteers blossom in the company of other people's miseries. In this way, the problems of one region become representative of an entire continent. These people always talk about helping 'children in Africa' as if children the entire continent over need help. By reinforcing stereotypes on social media posts, they often lean into racist analogies during their engagement with children, then retreat into white fragility when confronted. This means that the very people who are the focus of their actions are pushed to the margins.

Children are obviously delighted to receive goodies from their 'savior'. Even though the goodies are fleeting, the confidence and hope that volunteers promote is that of "we are changing the lives of African children". When back at home, they tell tall tales of a continent wrecked but beautiful and in this way they can peddle the 'redeemer of poor Africans' narrative.

Poverty porn vs. empowerment:

A balance between money and mission

Volunteerism is becoming a multibillion dollar industry; an industry we see doing more harm than good to local communities. As we all know, Africa is a diverse continent, with individual countries of huge diversity with to a large extent, diverse local communities. Voluntourism takes place in an environment where knowledge and insight into this diversity is virtually non-existent with volunteers applying a 'one shoe fits all' approach. They do not understand the diverse local cultures, languages, economy or rich traditions of the place they are visiting. Volunteers often put little premium in preparing themselves for their noble course.

To put things into perspective, I am not generalizing regarding all forms of volunteering; neither dismissing the invaluable contribution of humanitarian aid. I am also not trying to paint a negative picture towards every single person volunteering in good faith in Africa; instead I am trying to present a contextual overview and offering some suggestions.

So here are my thoughts. It would seem that there is an innate need for a paradigm shift in order for the objectives of volunteerism to go beyond pleasing donors and to uphold the noble nature of the mission. The volunteers should, even briefly, walk in the shoes of the local community they are about to help.

In 2012, Nigerian-American author, Teju Cole, coined the term 'White Saviour Industrial Complex following the release of the documentary film, Kony 2012. Cole defines White saviour industrial complex (WSIC) as "the confluence of practices, processes and institutions that reify historical inequalities to ultimately validate white privilege. WSIC entails a wider emotional engagement that validates privilege." [114]

Well-intentioned but Naive Volunteers

Reinforcing Stereotypes

The many distorted images of Africa pave the way for the White messiah complex. As Cole puts it, it creates a need for white intervention for "emotional needs to be satisfied" so the opportunity for agency at the local or individual level becomes non-existent.

Ultimately, celebrity largesse largely takes the form of a cure without a proper diagnosis. Without an understanding of the root cause and complexity of the problems in Africa, of the complexity and diversity of the continent and generalizing its problems into a single unit, the cause will definitely be hampered. .

There is much more to 'doing good' than making a difference. Those in need should be part of the process, should be consulted and be partners and not only recipients. A paradigm shift is profoundly needed, otherwise white savior complex will remain unchallenged and omnipresent.

Culture Appropriation: Blackfishing as a Culture Trope

Live ammunition for the socially-conscious

THERE HAVE BEEN NUMEROUS discussions regarding cultural appropriation by white people from the sporting of cornrows to critiques on the rampant commercialization of Kizumba. Fashion or fun is often cited as justification for this cultural appropriation. There is of course, nothing wrong with dancing Kizumba, it is owning it that is the problem and the line between appreciation and appropriation is often blurred.

It is possible to appreciate other cultures without appropriating them.

It is very common nowadays for people to hide behind political correctness whenever an important issue is raised. Cultural appropriation is one of these issues which rarely sits outside the political correctness conundrum and is indeed, often dismissed because the world has become a global village and therefore people are sharing or adopting new cultures. Whilst this is undoubtedly a fact, there is however, more than just this abstract way of looking at globalization. The interplay between the legacy of colonialism, the ubiquitous white supremacy ideology and globalization play a significant role in understanding the impact of cultural appropriation on many Black people.

The perceived supremacy of Western civilization has produced a cultural hierarchy by which Western culture sits at the top. This hierarchy has cross-fertilized worldwide to a point that even non-whites value Western culture as a standard currency. The same applies to beauty whereby white people set standards of beauty that the rest of the world follows. We see a lot of skin bleaching among darker-skinned individuals, women wearing long Brazilian wigs, a rise in double eye surgery and blue contact lenses among Chinese women. These cultural and aesthetic references are embedded in white western culture. This is the colonial legacy that we face in Africa where Western culture is more revered than our own.

In the African context, it is more to do with self-loathing or mental slavery, a colonial relic that is still prevalent in the continent. Some Black women feel they have to wear long wigs because their natural afro hair is considered dirty, messy and unprofessional. Conversely, we also see many Black women articulating their Blackness, owning it and becoming confident about it.

It is imperative to appreciate other cultures. In fact, we often share cultures whether it is food, language, cutlery or apparels, some we cannot do without especially when living in the Diaspora. However, applying a double standard is symptomatic of prejudice and ownership. For instance, there have been many of cases where Black students with dreadlocks have been suspended from school; a Blackman with dreadlocks is often seen as a thug or a drug-user whereas a white person with dreadlocks is a fashionista. It represents a double standard when it comes to Black people and their hair, particularly in relation to women.

It is common to see a white person wearing African attire while at the same time looking down upon Africans; or a white lady wearing cornrows but is racist. Why should someone appropriate the elements of other cultures and at the same time exhibit prejudicial tendencies towards the very culture he or she plagiarises? It is a continuation of a colonial ownership mindset blended with economic oppression of the disadvantaged culture.

I strongly believe that people should share and at the same time appreciate other cultures. Only then, shall we be able to understand and respect each other regardless of our physical differences. I cannot fathom the idea that there is a higher percentage of other cultures that are interested in using other cultures as an accessory whilst disrespecting them. In this case, the significance of a minority culture is reduced to mere costume, something just for fun. It is ok for a white person to wear African attire but only if he or she understands and respects the culture behind the attire.

Culture as Costume

Celebrities aka Instagram influencers have been caught in this web of cultural appropriation. It is a grandiose façade, where a number of celebrities have been accused of altering their features to look like Black women; with darker skin, fuller lips, bigger bums, braids and sometimes curls. It is interesting how beauty can transition and where Black women's features become the envy of white women. These are people who take advantage of their borrowed physical ambiguity to present themselves to brands that use them to represent diversity. These types of women are dishonestly positioning themselves as Black women and endeavoring to be influencers.

The *Oxford Dictionary defines 'cultural appropriation' as an unacknowledged or inappropriate adoption of the customs, practices, ideas, etc. of one people or society by members of another and typically more dominant people or a society.*

To put it plainly, it is when an individual adopts elements of a culture that is not his or her own such as a hairstyle, a piece of clothing, a way of speaking etc. Unlike cultural exchange where individuals mutually exchange their cultures, culture appropriation often plays a role in power dynamics where members of a dominant culture appropriate from a disadvantaged minority group.

Even though there is nothing wrong with adopting elements of a culture other than one's own, whether it's being in time for a meeting or making pizza or sushi, let us not confuse cultural exchange with its appropriation. It becomes a contentious issue when a dominant group takes from the culture of an oppressed group. The bottom line is that the marginalised group does not have a say in when their culture is being owned by an individual of dominant power and privilege, either for fun or just fashion. The privileged become its owners. In other words, a situation where one pretends to be a race without calling into play stereotypes to do so.

Is it equally wrong for a minority group to do the same? Yes, this applies, although in a different trajectory. In most cases, minority or marginalised groups adopt the culture of a dominant group in order to be part of society, in a process of integration and acculturation and more of assimilation.

Cultural appropriation is a controversial topic that requires a deeper understanding. A large number of people are still perplexed and fail to understand its implications, given that we live in a globalised world where cultures influence each other. People who share a common space of diversity are likely to exchange or share some elements of their cultures such as dialect, customs, traditions or even religion.

To be clear, cultural appropriation has nothing to do with familiarity with another culture. It is entirely a process by which a dominant group exploits the culture of a less privileged group. In most cases, this occurs within the premise of racial lines oblivious to history, experience and traditions; a history that means that many white people see Black people as lesser human beings. And it is at this moment that the culture becomes more valued than the humanity that produced it.

Borrowing would be a better term to refer to cultural appropriation. Take for instance rock and roll that was actually created by Black people in the 1950s. Due to segregation during that time, White record executives decided to have white artists replicate the sound of Black musicians. Nowadays, rock and roll is synonymous with whiteness. They took it and owned it.

Another victim in the music industry is twerking, a type of dance predominant in the African-American community with its roots in some parts of Africa. Musicians like Millie Cyrus have been criticised for appropriating twerking.

Some elements of culture such as arts and music that originated with a minority group become subjugated by a dominant group. As a consequence the dominant group is seen as creative while the less privileged group continues to experience negative stereotyping, which can include assertions of a lack of intelligence and creativity. As the old adage goes, 'one's meat is another's poison'. The same applies to cultural appropriation. What one individual considers an accolade, members of that group or community may consider disrespectful. It is a blurred line that must be cautiously and selflessly deliberated.

Cultural appropriation remains a problem and context is often the key. For instance, is a cultural element being adopted for its relevance or for fun? This sort of appropriation strips minority groups, the genuine cultural owners, of credit and merit.

It is without doubt that every individual has the freedom to make choices on how they want to relate or connect with others. Most individuals of a dominant group are not cognizant of the harm that culture appropriation inflicts unless he/she is criticised.

Some common sense should come into play here before one digs into the culture of others. You should ask yourself the following questions;

What is your true intention? Are you motivated by an authentic interest in that culture or just sheer fashion? How do you respect this culture and how do you think your appropriation will affect the community?

Showing an authentic interest in other cultures is not something that should be a concession. That is the most important part of diversity. However, it is the motive that stands out and makes people become apprehensive. It is not a question of whether white people seek permission to have fun, but the discounted interest in reinforcing a racial history of dominance, oppression and exploitation. Something to consider is that not everyone who borrows from another's culture is a coloniser or an oppressor in disguise. Some people are just ignorant.

Blackface: The changing faces of White Supremacy

EVERY YEAR, AS EUROPEANS and Americans prepare to celebrate Halloween, the issue of blackface often finds its way into conversations. Halloween is often a reminder that the big elephant in the room is yet to be 'seen'. People who understand that blackface is insidious are at loggerheads with proponents of blackface who believe that it is just a costume and that Black people are too sensitive to issues that are no longer relevant.

There are those who would say that they are not racist so it is fine for them to paint their face black during Halloween. Whether it is Halloween or in a football stadium or on Three Kings Day in Spain, White people blacking their faces have always been a divisive tradition. It is part of a history of dehumanization. Whereby racist history is swept under the carpet or hidden behind a facade of ignorance. There have been widespread claims of ignorance by white celebrities, college students and government officials across Europe when confronted about this matter.

The genesis of Blackface in Europe and in the rest of the world is rooted in America's first cultural export by a man named Thomas Dartmouth Rice. Rice was the creator of the Minstrel shows in Europe in 1836 where white performers depicted African-American slaves in shredded clothes, dancing and singing songs such as "Jump Jim Crow". Thereafter the minstrel shows extended to Australia, India, South America, South

Africa and to the rest of the world. These shows percolated the ideas and images of Blackface to other cultures[115].

So why is Blackface so contentious? Is it just another costume like for Halloween or is there more to it than that?

Blackface is more than just the painting of white skin a dark colour. Historically, it is a practise that dates back some 200 years. Blackface was a practice by which Black people were mocked for the entertainment of white people and negative stereotypes were entrenched across the US and Europe. In the early 19th century, White actors known as minstrel performers would paint their faces and perform thoroughly racist, allegedly comedic routines about Black people as stage entertainment. They would mock Black people's accents, for instance. These portrayals were beyond parody, imprecise, degrading, hurtful and deeply insulting. However, many white people considered it a perfectly acceptable form of entertainment. This was done against the backdrop of a society that systematically enslaved and murdered Black people. At this particular time, Black people had no chance of getting a role in the entertainment industry because of their skin colour.

Blackface has been a longstanding issue in Europe where Black people are subjugated. As many have argued, blackfacing and mocking Black people, allowed White people to further subjugate Black people whilst perpetuating a sense of superiority.

The United Nations working group of experts on People of African Descent upon completing their visit to Belgium in 2019 gave the following media statement;

> *The use of blackface, racialized caricatures and racist representations of people of African descent is offensive, dehumanizing and contemptuous. Regrettably, the republication of 'Tintin in the Congo', unedited and without contextualization, perpetuates negative stereotypes and the book should be either withdrawn or contextualized with an addendum reflecting current commitments to anti-racism. Stereotypes of people of African descent that are rooted in enslavement, colonization and neo-colonialism characterize the harmful image conveyed by the media. Such images are accompanied by a devaluation of African people – a devaluation of that which is African. Racist insults and other clichés accentuate the phenomenon[116].*

Even though several anti-discrimination movements fought hard and succeeded for the removal of blackfacing in the entertainment industry, its usage is still presenting modern day Europe. Many activists, particularly of African descent have been vocal in naming and shaming institutions and individuals that show tendencies to blackface even though it might not be entirely blatant blackfacing.

Early in 2019, Katy Perry removed two items from her shoe range after many people complained that one of the designs was racist. The shoes in Katy's collections were said to resemble blackface images, with black leather faces, blue eyes and red lips.

The prevalence of blackface in Europe is found in the least expected institutions. For Christians, Christmas is a season of forgiveness and benevolence, however, in some countries, this season is marred by controversy.

In the Netherlands, the 5th of December is a celebration of the day that Santa arrives with his helper, Black Pete. If children have been badly behaved Black Pete kidnaps them. During the parades, Black Pete is always a white man in blackface. In November 2019, the Dutch Saint Nicholas parade replaced Blackface with 'sooty faces' following a spate of debates and protests. Black Pete has also taken a different twist in Europe with adults wearing gaudy costumes, large gold earrings, afro-style wigs, red lipstick and full blackface make-up. Many critics see the event as racist and as depicting slavery[117].

During the Christmas period, in Spain, there is also a tradition of white people blackening their faces to portray one of the three wise men. In fact the UN Working Group of experts on People of African Descent were told by representatives of civil society and people of African descent, during their country visit to Spain in 2018 that the festivities using blackface were considered an offensive, insulting and dehumanising caricature of people of African descent. In Catalonia and in Alcoy in Alicante province, the Working Group was told about the depiction of a blackface in the Cabalgata de los Reyes Magos (Cavalcade of the Magi) and the depiction of wooden giants with black faces in the city of Tarragona during the festival of Santa Tecla[118]

This tradition is also practised in Germany where recently, a German jury termed blackface the new Anglicism. During the Three Wise Men event, Catholic children in Germany dress up as Magi going from door to door singing and asking for money for charity. One of the Magi often paints his face to represent Melchior[119].

Canadian Prime Minister Justine Trudeau in 2019 apologised after an old photo of him revealed him dressed as an Arab prince. In the photo Mr. Trudeau has darkened the skin on his face and hands. He admitted that the photo was racist and regretted that even though it was many years ago, 'he should have known better.[120].

In sport, football clubs in particular have been marred by the blackfacing by fans. We still recall the 2018 Football World Cup when German football fans blackfaced during the Germany vs. Ghana march. It was a move that drew attention prompted FIFA to open an investigation into racism. In stark contrast, German team Deinster SV, blackfaced to make a stance on racism and show solidarity with one of its team members, Emad Babiker, who had been the victim of a racially motivated attack. In this case, the team made an unorthodox move by flipping the intention of blackfacing and using it to raise awareness and show solidarity[121].

Whilst some players were taking a stand in an act of considered decency, one player a thousand miles away became caught up in controversy. In December 2017, Atletico Madrid forward

Antoine Griezmann was criticised for painting his skin to dress up as a black basketball player.[122]

Many people do not understand that the concept of blackface is not about merely painting the skin black but that it goes far beyond that. Most people who have been involved in blackface incidents and then apologised have often cited their lack of awareness. However, not having an understanding of the agonizing and appalling history of blackface cannot be a justification.

The reality is that even if one does not think of the racist implications of wearing blackface, it does not in any way change the impact and effect on those who see it. The excuse of not being cognizant of the consequences of one's behaviour, is an archetypal constituent of privilege and power.

It is not only whites who practise blackface, coloured people have also reinforced this prejudice. In 2017, a Malaysian beauty chain sparked furious allegations of racism when it depicted a woman with 'blackface' as being undesirable[123].

In 2018, as every year when China celebrates the new Lunar year, there was a TV show featuring a woman in blackface with exaggerated buttocks. Later in the same year, a TV actor in Kuwait apologised for appearing in a show with blackface to depict Sudanese people[124].

Toxic History: Eugenics in Eastern Central Europe

HUMANITY HAS BEEN THIRSTY for perfection; for being healthy, beautiful and intelligent. Indeed, in reality, it would be rare to have a single soul with all these characteristics. Probably this thirst is what has inspired the invention of robots and artificial intelligence. We have seen scientists endeavour to create species that perfectly meet the above criteria. This may also account for the breeding of animals for a specific trait.

Eugenics is a practice and belief that human genetics can be improved upon by excluding people of inferior race and traits whilst promoting those considered superior. This was the most deplorable aspect of eugenics both morally and politically. Eugenics, supported by convincing research, promised to grow healthier and wiser people[125].

Eugenics has a toxic history of race and science where white people believed that since they were the dominant group, they were also the best and should continue with world domination.

Eugenics is still alive and kicking today and there are several ways of identifying its traits. For example, the British Prime Minister Boris Johnson's former top adviser, Andrew Sabisky, a self-proclaimed political "forecaster", argued that forced long-term contraception might help tackle the problem of a "permanent underclass". He also suggested that Black people are less intelligent than white people.[126]

Eugenics is not something that anyone can now seriously embrace; we need only look back less than 100 years ago when Hitler applied this ideology to justify the murder of millions of human beings.

As Western civilization progressed, some scientists felt there was need to 'advance' humanity. Francis Galton, the godfather of eugenics became a driving force in this quest. Galton was a British scientist studying obituaries, family histories and creating family trees. He hypothesised that high intelligence and other noble characteristics are hereditary. In 1883, he recommended that humanity should be improved, encouraging the 'best' members of the society to have more children so that the good traits of their parents could proliferate. He worked on statistics, heredity and evolution, and his pioneering technique on fingerprints are still used. Charles Darwin's work had had a great influence on Galton. Darwin's theory of the survival of the fittest had been widely contested and was seen as a propagator of white supremacy[127].

Even though there is little discourse on the prevalence of eugenics in Eastern and Central Europe, research has shown that as early as 1900, eugenics literature was already circulating in the region and that influential eugenicist theories were already available in the university libraries of Vienna, Prague, Budapest and Bucharest. Eugenics research was already being conducted and institutionalized in Prague as early as 1913. Later in the same year, socio-biology and eugenics became established in Vienna within the Sociology Library.

Having two eugenics societies and other institutions advancing research to improve the health of the population, Hungarians became trailblazers in eugenics in central and Eastern Europe[128]. The Czechs and Poles also engaged in a corresponding position during the 1920s and by the 1930s, Austria, Czechoslovakia, Poland, Hungary and Yugoslavia became members of the International Federation of Eugenics Organizations (IFEO), whilst Romania became prominent in the international Federation of Latin Eugenic Societies, founded in Mexico City in October 1935[129].

Due to its geographical and political influence, German racial hygiene cross-fertilized within the region. Without doubt, German racial hygiene was of great interest in East Central Europe, among eugenicists such as Austrian dermatologist Rudolf Polland (1876-1952), the Hungarian diplomat Geza Hoffman (1885-1921), the Saxon physician Heinrich Siegmund (1867-1937) and the Romanian neurologist Gheorghe Marinescu (1863-1938). American and French eugenics were equally influential especially in Czech, Hungary and Romania[130].

Europe has had distressing periods in its history; with two world wars and a robust chain of inter-war geographical, social and national changes with a variety of political systems; from imperial to republican in Austria; a democratic populist government in Czechoslovakia; federalist in Yugoslavia; as well as authoritarian in Poland and Hungary. In the case of Romania and Croatia, this inter-war period resulted in the outright fascist regimes of the 1940s. Even more dreadful, between 1938 and 1945 the three countries of Austria, Czechoslovakia and Poland ceased to exist as sovereign states with parts of Yugoslavia (now Slovenia) being annexed by Nazi Germany.[131]

At the end of World War I, East Central Europe crumbled. New governments implemented different forms of controlling its citizens in line with new nation-state ideologies and social institutions. The eugenicist obsession with fertility and marriage and the portrayal of the nation as an arm of family became tangled and incongruous[132].

Undoubtedly, eugenics created a sort of paradigm shift regarding how the state and minorities related to each other. Eugenics succeeded in constructing a variation in physical and cultural differences that resulted in the categorization of who should be referred to as a majority and a minority. Dr. Magdalena Gawin, the author of 'Race and Modernity: a History of the Polish Eugenics Movement', explains that human life was valued according to the criteria of health, race, education, social and property status. The government pointed to the state budget burdens caused by the care of terminally ill children, children with mental retardation, the elderly, disabled and people who were afraid that their diseases were hereditary[133].

Darwin's theory of evolution with the first publication *On The Origin of Species* in 1859, Mendel's law of inheritance and Galton's proposal for artificial race selection laid the foundation for the progress of eugenicist ideology in the twentieth century. Since its inception, Darwin's theory has lived up to expectations, with many scientists, commentators and politicians openly embracing it[134].

In 1869, Galton published the work, *'Hereditary Genius'* where he presented the basic problems studied by the science that he later called eugenics. He argued that the development prospects of any civilization depended on the condition of the race. The more outstanding individuals in a given race, the better the civilization would develop. He also believed that talent for politics, sports, and poetry-writing were inherited in much the same way as skin and eye colour. As with talents, so negative traits such as physical and mental retardation, along with gravitation towards crime and cruelty were also subject to the process of heredity. This is why Galton argued that the reproductive rights of families burdened with bad heredity should be limited. He warned however that not all selection measures would bring about desired results. Sometimes a race had hereditary traits which were irremovable. In this case, he prophesied, such races would be 'supplanted and replaced by their better'[135].

In 1883, he published a book *'Inquiries into Human Faculties,'* where he underlined the existence of a social hierarchy as a natural vindication of the fitter and stronger. Galton believed that most people were characterised by low intellectual and moral standards that impeded the progress of civilization. Therefore, control should be taken over the process of human evolution by deliberately supporting the fittest and most worthy individuals[136].

This was a task that he assigned to the new science of eugenics. In his book, Galton criticized traditional charity and philanthropy. He believed that 'emotional humanitarianism' ignored the laws of evolution and interfered with natural selection, increasing the number of degenerate individuals. He proposed giving assistance to the stronger rather than the weak and healthy rather than the sick and to think about the future rather than the present[137].

A nightmare that Few Remember Today

In Poland, there has been only scant discourse about eugenics and it is largely a history that has been swept under the carpet. In 2008, the University of Warsaw library held an exhibition of 200 photos and several archival documents, several dozen posters and exhibits including original anthropological instruments and measuring cards from racial anthropological research from the inter-war years, as well as documentary and feature films depicting the strong scientific basis of eugenics[138].

The Polish eugenics movement was also influenced by German eugenics, known also as racial hygiene (*Ressenhygiene*). The German eugenics movement dated back to the 1890s. One may discern four principle stages in its development: the formative stage (1890-1903), racial hygiene in Wilhelmine Germany (1904-1918), in the Welmar Republic (1918-1933) and Nazi racial hygiene (1933-1939 and 1939-1944). Three contexts need to be taken into consideration while analysing German eugenics/racial hygiene. These are:-the social problems result from rapid industrialization; the character and traditions of the German medical community and the attractiveness of the 'selective' variant of social Darwinism for German naturalists, physicists and social theorists[139].

In a 2019 radio interview, Father Tadeusz Rydzik, one of the most vocal and influential Catholic priests, discouraged Polish people from entering into 'mixed marriages saying that Poles should not marry people from other countries. He additionally conflated culture, language and religion with immigration efforts intended to preserve white homogeneity. He lambasted mixed marriages, citing cases where Polish women had been attracted to the darker skin of an Arab but that once they had married, the real drama began and that marriage should not be based on hormones and emotions[140].

Father Rydzyk owns a radio and TV station where he serves as a director. In these ways, Rydzik's narrative echoes the premises of the eugenics movement.

Racial hygiene

Eugenics took the West by storm (like a fashion magazine). Eugenics societies were founded, journals dedicated to its ideology were published, international conferences organized and even government agencies established to advance the movement. Needless to say eugenics quickly became an instrument for politicians.

Several programs of forced sterilization and castration of people with disabilities, with genetic defects and those considered inferior came into force. In the US, about 60,000 people and a similar number in Sweden became the victims of eugenics. The same practices, although on a smaller scale, took place in Finland, Norway, Denmark, Japan, Switzerland, Canada, Latvia and Iceland. Many treatments were carried out on the basis of superficial justifications, in which there were often manifestations of racial and ideological prejudices[141].

Scientists estimate that during the Nazist Reich, more than 400,000 people became the victims of forced sterilization. The decisions were made by "hereditary health courts", initially dealing mainly with patients, as well as reaching ethnic minorities and children from mixed marriages[142]. This number may be higher since most of the sterilizations of mixed race individuals were not well documented.

Scientific racism with political aspirations

Eugenics was a form of scientifically justified racism in the sense that it was meant to improve the condition of one race by improving the physical and mental properties of the human body, mobilizing scientists from various fields such as statisticians, psychologists, psychiatrists, anthropologists and geneticists. It was predicated upon the discrimination of some people using science as a vehicle. We can see the consequences of Nazi racial hygiene during the Holocaust and after the Second World War.

The Polish eugenics movement began in the early 20th century, founded by a doctor of venereology, Leon Wernic. He was a member of an elite world of Polish scientists. It is estimated that, towards the end of World War I, the Polish Eugenics

Society had about 10,000 members. In the years 1934-1938, Polish eugenics proposed several bills on social policy which included sterilization, coercion, prohibition of marriages of sick and disabled persons and other measures aimed at eliminating people considered inferior[143].

The Nazis ideologised eugenics as the scientific rationalization for genocide of the disabled, Jews, Gypsies and Slavs, all with the intention of preserving a pure Germanic race. This is one of the most depressing phenomena of the 20th century that is being almost entirely forgotten but is valid proof of the contemporary problem of racism, white supremacy, discrimination and prejudice.

Even though the Communist regime disbanded the eugenics movement, its ideological remnants are still present in modern Central and Eastern Europe.

ANNEX

Fig. 1.

A list compiled by Deutsche Welle highlighting some of the books deemed racist[144].

'The Little Witch' (1957)

A classic of children's literature, by Otfried Preussler, which was made into a film that came out earlier this year. In a 2013 revision of the book, children getting dressed up as a "Neger" — a derogatory word that can either be translated as "negro" or "nigger" — or a "Zigeuner" (gypsy) simply picked other costumes. The publisher's decision to change some words led to a heated debate in Germany.

'The Little Ghost' (1966)

The Thienemann publishing house decided to review Preussler's other classic children's books including "The Robber Hotzenplotz" books and "The Little Ghost" (made into a film in 2013). They reformulated for example the friendly ghost's reaction when he turns black. Such revisions shocked purists: Should books be changed? And where should the line be drawn?

'Jim Button and Luke the Engine Driver' (1960)

Experts view Michael Ende's popular children's novel as an allegory against the Nazis ideology. During his lifetime, the author updated his book, turning references to China into a fictional country called Mandala. However, the latest edition maintains the term 'Neger', used once to describe the Black boy in the tale. The latest movie adaption of the work was recently released in cinemas (photo).

The 'Pippi Longstocking' series

The word 'negro' was already removed or replaced from the English version of Astrid Lindgren's popular books during the 1950s. The German version had been reworked in the 1990s; however, it kept the term with a footnote mentioning that it was outdated. In 2009, all references to Pippi's dad as the "Negerkönig" (Negro King) were replaced with the 'South Sea King.

'The Story of Doctor Doolittle' (1920)

Hugh Lofting's classic was reworked for its 1988 edition; instead of coming from the "Land of the White Men," Doctor Dolittle is from the "Land of the Europeans." Similarly, references to the King of Jolliginki avoid mentioning the color of his skin. Despite efforts to make race invisible, the colonial ideologies of the time are still reflected in the plot and the depictions of the characters.

'Charlie and the Chocolate Factory' (1964)

In the original version of Roald Dahl's book, the Oompa-Loompas, small humans working in Willy Wonka's chocolate factory, are described as African Pygmies. The author had them come from a fictional country called Loompaland in a revised edition from 1973. In the 1971 film (photo), they were played by actors with dwarfism and depicted as surreal creatures with orange skin and green hair.

'And Then There Were None' (1939)

The original title of Agatha Christie's masterpiece was "Ten Little Niggers," based on the British blackface song that guides the plot of the mystery novel. The title of the US edition, published a month later used the last five words of the song instead. However, it also had the problematic title, "Ten Little Indians," which refers to an American rhyming song.

'Tintin in the Congo' (1946)

Initially published as a serialized weekly in the 1930s, Belgian cartoonist Herge later produced a color version of the work and revised one violent, big-game hunting scene in 1976. By the late 1990's, the volume was strongly criticized for its racist content and there have been attempts to ban the book. In English editions it is sold with an additional explanation of the historical context.

'Adventures of Huckleberry Finn' (1884)

Mark Twain's iconic classic is viewed as an anti-racist satire. It is also among the first American works to use vernacular English and coarse language. The word "nigger," a common racial slur in the mid-19th-century, is used over 200 times in the book. One revised version from 2011 replaces the N-word with "slave." Critics believe it is wrong to whitewash the historical context of such books[145].

Fig. 2

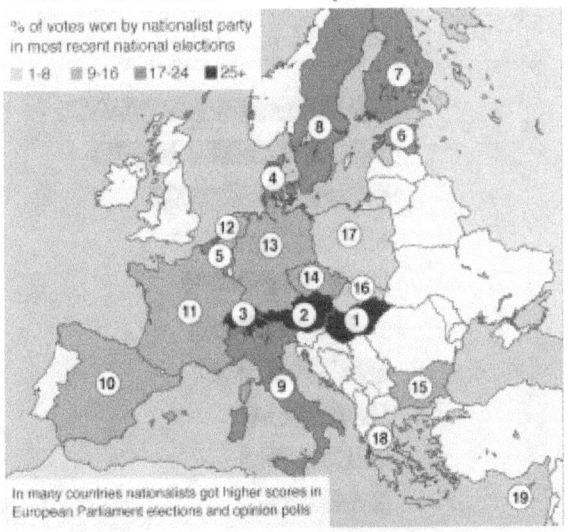

Rise of nationalism in Europe

% of votes won by nationalist party in most recent national elections

◼ 1-8   ◼ 9-16   ◼ 17-24   ◼ 25+

In many countries nationalists got higher scores in European Parliament elections and opinion polls

1. **Hungary**
   Fidesz 49% Jobbik 19%

2. **Austria**
   Freedom Party 26%

3. **Switzerland**
   Swiss People's Party 25.8%

4. **Denmark**
   Danish People's Party 21%

5. **Belgium**
   New Flemish Alliance 20.4%

6. **Estonia**
   Conservative People's Party 17.8%

7. **Finland**
   The Finns 17.7%

8. **Sweden**
   Sweden Democrats 17.6%

9. **Italy**
   The League 17.4%

10. **Spain**
    Vox 15%

11. **France**
    National Rally 13%

12. **Netherlands**
    Freedom Party 13%

13. **Germany**
    Alternative for Germany 12.6%

14. **Czech Republic**
    Freedom & Direct Democracy 11%

15. **Bulgaria**
    United Patriots 9%

16. **Slovakia**
    Our Slovakia 8%

17. **Poland**
    Confederation 6.8%

18. **Greece**
    Greek Solution 3.7%

19. **Cyprus**
    ELAM 3.7%

Last updated: May 2019   BBC

https://www.bbc.com/news/world-europe-36130006

Fig. 4

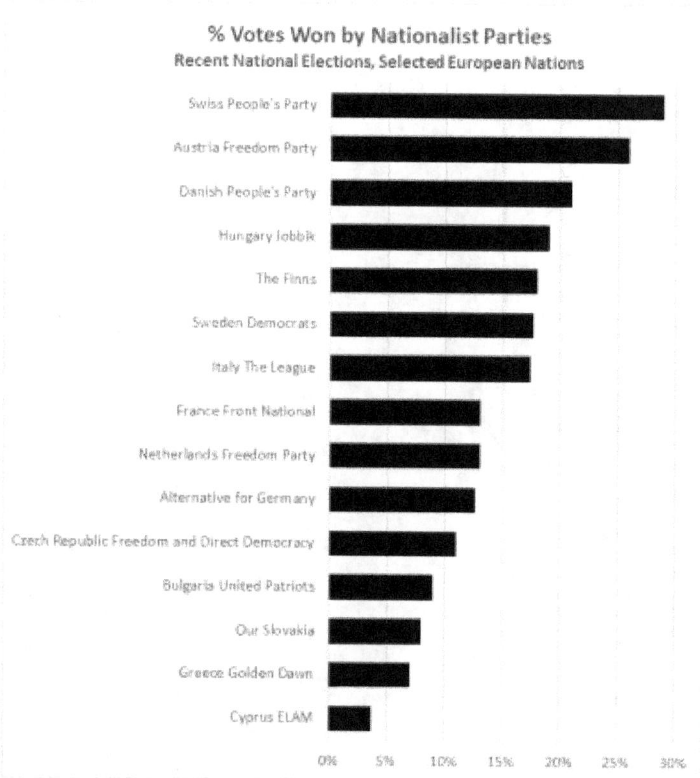

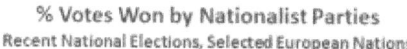

% Votes Won by Nationalist Parties
Recent National Elections, Selected European Nations

Swiss People's Party	
Austria Freedom Party	
Danish People's Party	
Hungary Jobbik	
The Finns	
Sweden Democrats	
Italy The League	
France Front National	
Netherlands Freedom Party	
Alternative for Germany	
Czech Republic Freedom and Direct Democracy	
Bulgaria United Patriots	
Our Slovakia	
Greece Golden Dawn	
Cyprus ELAM	

0%   5%   10%   15%   20%   25%   30%

HTTPS://YALEGLOBAL.yale.edu/content/bbc-news-europe-and-nationalism[2]

2. https://yaleglobal.yale.edu/content/bbc-news-europe-and-nationalism

Fig. 4

Selected list of recent information (2014-2015) regarding the cases of people who died at the hands of the police in the UK:

● Azelle Rodney was shot dead by an armed officer from the Metropolitan Police on 30 April 2005. On 3 July 2015, the officer that shot him was found not guilty by a majority verdict.

● Sean Rigg, who suffered from paranoid schizophrenia, died following a cardiac arrest after being arrested and forcibly restrained on 21 August 2008 while in police custody in Brixton. The two officers, whose evidence under oath about Rigg's death was contradicted by CCTV evidence, did not face criminal charges.

● Mark Duggan was shot and killed by the police on 4 August 2011 on suspicion of planning an attack and being in possession of a handgun. The circumstances of his death were one of the major causes for the 2011 riots. In January 2014, an inquest found that Duggan was "lawfully killed", despite being unarmed.

● Stephen Lawrence was murdered by a group of up to six White youths in a racially motivated attack in 1993. It took more than 18 years to bring two of his killers to justice. Commander Richard Walton who was removed from operational duties due to discreditable conduct in relation to the Lawrence case later resumed his role.

• Jimmy Mubenga died on board a plane as he was being deported from the UK back to Angola on 12 October 2010. On 16 December 2014, the three guards who restrained and ultimately choked him to death were found not guilty of Mr. Mubenga's manslaughter

Source: Afrophobia in Europe. ENAR shadow report 2014-2015.

BIBLIOGRAPHY

1. The Washington Post, August 28,2018
2. Ali Rattansi. Racism; A Very Short Introduction. Oxford University Press. 2007
3. Albert Memmi, Racism. An introduction by Steve Martinit pg 18. University of Minnesota. 2000
4. George M Fredrickson. Racism, a short history. Princeton University Press, 2002
5. George L. Mosse. Toward the Final Solution. The University of Wisconsin Press. 1978,1985
6. EU-MIDIS II, second European Union Minorities and Discrimination survey, Being Black in the EU, 2018.   file:///C:/Users/Jimmy/Desktop/book/Embargoed_Being_Black_in_the_EU_embargoed.pdf
7. Afromagazine.nl/nieuws/black-people-are-increasingly-attacked-while-europe-responds-impunity-and-indifference
8. Todd D. Nelson, A Handbook of Prejudice, Stereotyping and Discrimination. Psychology Press, a Taylor and Francis Group. 2009.
9. George Yancy. What White Looks Like. Routledge, Network and London. 2004
10. Luigi Luca Cavalli-Sforza, Paolo Menozzi, and Alberto Piazza, *The History and Geography of Human Genes* (Princeton, NJ: Princeton University Press, 1994).
11. Richard S. Cooper, Jay S. Kaufman, and Ryk Ward, "Race and Genomics," *New England Journal of*

Medicine 348, no. 12 (2003): 1166–70.

12. Robin DiAngelo, White Fragility. Why It's Hard for White People to Talk About Racism. Forward by Michael Eric Dyson Beacon Press, Boston. 2018.

13. Eduardo Bonilla-Silva. Racism without Racists, Colour-blind racism and the persistence of racial inequality in the United States, 2006

14. Cherryl Harris 1993

15. Ruth Frankenberg 1997

16. https://www.nytimes.com/2018/03/31/world/europe/denmark-statue-black-woman.html

17. George .M. Fredrick. Racism a short history. Princeton University Press. 2002

18. George Yancy. Look a White, Philosophical essays on Whiteness. Temple University Press, 2012.

19. Race and Science; Racial myths. New York Columbia,1961

20. Nationalism, Peter Alter,1985

21. Maik Fielitz, Laura LotteLaloire, The trouble on the far right, contemporary right wing strategies and practices in Europe. 2016

22. Challenges to democracies in East Central Europe, Jan Holzer, Miroslav mares, Routledge

23. Ernest Gellner. New perspectives on the past. Nations and nationalism. Basil Blackwell. 1983.

24. Harold D. Fishbein. Peer prejudice and discrimination, the origins of prejudice, second edition. University of Cincinnati. Lawrence Erlbaum associates, publishers, malwah, New jersey. 2002.

25. Andrzej Marcin Suszycki and Ireneusz Pawel

Karolewski. Nationalism in contemporary Europe: Is there still anything to explore? Edinburg University press, 2011.

26. Joseph Rothschild, Nancy M. Wingfield. Return to diversity, a political history of east Central Europe since World War II. Oxford University Press. 2000.

27. Joshua Glasgow. A theory of race. Routledge. 2009.

28. K. Anthony Appiah, Amy Gutman. Colour conscious, the political morality of race. Princeton University Press. 1999.

29. Malcolm X, the end of White world supremacy, four speeches, edited and with an introduction by Imam Benjamin Karim. Arcade publishing. 1971.

30. Mathew hughey. White bound, nationalists, antiracists, and the shared meanings of race. Stanford University Press. 2012.

31. Michael Bilig. Banal nationalism. SAGE publications. 2002.

32. Monica Shelley and Margret Winck. What is Europe, Aspects of European cultural diversity? Routledge. 2005.

33. Todd D. Nelson. A handbook of prejudice, stereotypes and discrimination

34. Gabriella Lazaradis, Giovanna Campani, Anne Benveniste. The rise of the far right in Europe, populist shift and othering. Palgrave Macmillan. 2016.

35. George Lipsitz. How racism takes place. Temple University Press, Philadelphia. 2011.

36. Encyclopaedia of Race and Racism, vol. a-f, John

Hartwell Moore, Editor in chief, Thomson Gaile, USA.2008

37. Sander L. Gilman, James M. Thomas. Are racists crazy? How prejudice, racism and anti-Semitism became markers of insanity. New York University Press, 2016.

38. Jane H. Hill. The everyday language of White racism. Wiley Blackwell, 2008.

39. Jeffrey Cole. The new racism in Europe, A Sicilian ethnography. Dowling College, New York, Cambridge University Press. 1997.

40. Tracy Baptiste. Character education: Overcoming prejudice. Chelsea house publishers, NY. 2009.

41. Pierr Andre Taguieff. The force of prejudice on racism and its doubles. Vol. 13. University of Minnesota press, Minneapolis. 2001.

42. Michaela Kotiig, Renate Bitzan, Andrea Peto. Gender and far right politics in Europe. Palgrave Macmillan. 2017

43. Peggy J Parks. How prevalent is racism in society. Reference Point Press, San Diego, CA. 2015.

44. Fascism, edited by Michael S. Neiberg, University of South Mississipi-hattiesburg, USA. Routledge. 2006

45. Karen S. Glover. Racial profiling, Research, Racism and Resistance. Rowman and Littlefield Publishers, INC. 2009.

46. Ian Law. Red racism: Racism in communist and post communist context. Palgrave Macmillan. 2012.

47. Peter A. J. Stevens. Ethnicity and racism in Cyprus, National pride and prejudice. Palgrave

macmillan.2016.

48. Minority integration in central and Eastern Europe, between ethnic division and equality. Edited and introduced by Timofey Agarin and maltebrosig. 2009.

49. Diversity and contestations over nationalism in Europe and Canada. Edited by John Erik Fossum, Riva Kastoryano and BirteSiim. Palgrave Macmillan. 2018.

50. Robert Miles and Malcolm brown. Racism, second edition. Routledge, London and New York. 2003

51. Antonio Costa Pinto. Corporatism and Fascism, The corporalist wave in Europe. Routledge. 2017.

52. Andre Gerritis. Nationalism in Europe since 1945. Palgrave Macmillan. 2016.

53. Cynthia Willia-Esqueda. Motivational aspects of prejudice and racism, vol. 53. Springer, 2008.

54. Alena Lentin. Racism and Anti racism in Europe. Pluto press. 2004.

55. Attila Melegh. On the East-West slope, Globalization, nationalism, racism and discourses on central and eastern Europe. CEU Press. 2006.

56. Irene V Blair. The malleability of automatic stereotypes and prejudice, University of Colorado at Boulder, Personality and social psychology review. 2002.

57. Charles King. Extreme politics. Nationalism, violence and the end of Eastern Europe. Oxford University press. 2010.

58. Charles W. Mills. The racial contract. Cornel

University press, Cithaca and London. 1997.

59. Christian Lammert, KatjaSarkowsky (Eds.). Travelling concept, negotiating diversity in Canada and Europe.VSVerlag Fur Sozialwissenschaften. 2010.

[1] The Washington post, August 28,2018

[2]https://www.politico.eu/article/toxic-news-refugees-migrants-eu/

[3]The rule of law in Poland and Hungary has worsened. Europarl.europa.eu.

[4] Bbc.com. Marine Le Pen: Taking France's National Front out of the Shadows. 7 May 2017

[5]https://www.politico.eu/article/toxic-news-refugees-migrants-eu/

[6]https://www.politico.eu/article/toxic-news-refugees-migrants-eu/

[7] Ali Rattansi. Racism; A Very Short Introduction, Oxford University Press. 2007

[8]Ibid

[9]Ibid

[10] Albert Memmi, Racism. An introduction by Steve Martinit pg 18. University of Minnesota. 2000

[11] Politico.eu. The fight to end unequal treatment of people of colour moves at a glacial pace in the EU.

[12] The guardian, As Italy's fist Black Minister, I suffered a vile racist abuse.

[13]bbc.com, Racism in France is a Latent Problem. 2013.

[14] Guardian.com. Black MEP claims he was asked to leave EU Parliament on first day, 7 July 2019.

[15] Ibid.

[16]https://www.thejournal.ie/german-minister-calls-singer-wonderful-negro-2304830-Sep2015/

[17] Afrophobia in Europe. ENAR Shadow Report, 2014-2015

[18] Ibid

[19]https://www.theguardian.com/media/2014/may/01/jeremy-clarkson-begs-forgiveness-n-word-top-gear

[20] BBC.com. Moussa Marega: Is football losing the fight against racism? 17 February 2020.

[21] BBC.com, Football Racism: You don't know what it's like. 12 Feb 2020

[22] Ibid

[23] Esme Nicholson, Morning Edition (NPR). 08/20/2018

[24] George M Fredrickson. Racism, a short history. Princeton University Press, 2002

[25]Ibid

[26] BBC.com. Belgium apology for mixed race kidnappings. 4 April 2019.link needed

[27] George L. Mosse. Toward the Final Soluon. The University of Wisconsin Press. 1978,1985.

[28] Being Black in the EU, Second European Union Minorities and Discrimination Survey. https://fra.europa.eu/en/publication/2018/being-black-eu

[29] Ibid

[30] Afrophobia in Europe. EANR shadow report 2014-2015.

[31] Afrophobia in Europe, EANR shadow report 2014-2015.

[32] Being Black in the EU, Second European Union Minorities and Discrimination Survey. https://fra.europa.eu/en/publication/2018/being-black-eu

[33] https://documents-dds-ny.un.org/doc/UNDOC/GEN/G19/243/13/PDF/G1924313.pdf?OpenElement

[34] Ibid

[35] Afrophobia in Europe. ENAR shadow report 2014-2015

[36] Lantern Slide 'Ten Little Nigger Boys Went Out to Dine'. The rhyme, written by Septimus Winner in 1868, was adapted in the late 1800s.It was a standard of the blackface minstrel shows and became widely known in Europe. It was used by Agatha Christie in her novel 'Ten Little Niggers' (1939)

[37] Being Black in the EU, Second European Union Minorities and Discrimination Survey. https://fra.europa.eu/en/publication/2018/being-black-eu

[38] Afromagazine.nl/nieuws/black-people-are-increasingly-attacked-while-europe-responds-impunity-and-indifference

[39] Aljazeera.com. Exploited, hated, killed@ The lives of African fruit pickers. 2018.

[40] Afrophobia in Europe. ENAR shadow report 2014-2015.

[41] Afrophobia in Europe. ENAR shadow report 2014-2015.

[42] Ibid.

[43]The Stephen Lawrence inquiry report by Sir William Macpherson of Cluny advised by Tom cook, the Right Reverend Dr John Sentamu, Dr Richard Stone. Presented to Parliament by the Secretary of State for the Home Department by Command of Her Majesty. February 1999. https://assets.publishing.service.gov.uk/government/uploads/system/uploads/attachment_data/file/277111/4262.pdf

[44] Fact.pl. A policeman killed a man in Warsaw. They dismissed the case. 2018

[45] Dw.com. New evidence contradicts German police in Oury Jalloh death, 2017.

[46]https://edge.ug/2020/02/26/scot-mum-takes-kids-to-uganda-to-show-them-real-poverty/

[47]John C. Brigham. The Role of Race and Racial Prejudice in Recognizing Other People, Motivational Aspects of Prejudice and Racism pp 68-110, 2008.

[48]Ali Rattansi, Racism, A Very Short Introduction, Oxford University Press. 2007

[49]Ibid

[50]Todd D. Nelson, A Handbook of Prejudice, Stereotyping and Discrimination. Psychology Press, a Tayor and Francis Group. 2009.

[51] https://www.enar-eu.org/Racist-crime-speech

[52]https://fra.europa.eu/en/publication/2018/hate-crime-recording-and-data-collection-practice-across-eu#TabPubFRAOpinionsandkeyfindings

[53]Carol Anderson 2016

[54]Afrohttp://www.red-network.eu/?i=red-network.en.items&id=652

[55]https://documents-dds-ny.un.org/doc/UNDOC/GEN/G19/243/13/PDF/G1924313.pdf?OpenElement

[56] George Yancy. What White Looks Like. Routledge, Network and London. 2004

[57]Ibid

[58] Luigi Luca Cavalli-Sforza, Paolo Menozzi, and Alberto Piazza, *The History and Geography of Human Genes* (Princeton, NJ: Princeton University Press, 1994).

[59] Richard S. Cooper, Jay S. Kaufman, and Ryk Ward, "Race and Genomics," *New England Journal of Medicine* 348, no. 12 (2003): 1166–70.

[60] Robin DiAngelo, White Fragility. Why it is so hard for white people to talk about racism. Forwarded by Michael Eric Dyson Beacon press, Boston. 2018.

[61] Eduardo Bonilla-Silva. Racism without Racists, Color-Blind Racism and the Persistence of Racial Inequality in the United States, 2006.

[62] Ali Mazrui. Shifting African identities: The boundaries of ethnicity and religion in Africa's experience. Pg 153. Volume II in the series: Identity? Theory, Politics and history. Human Science Research council, Pretoria, 2001

[63] Ibid. Pg.154

[64]Ibid pg. 9

[65]George Yancy. look a White, Philosophical Essays on Whiteness. Temple University Press, 2012.

[66]Robin DiAngelo, 2018

[67]Cheryl Harris, 1993

[68]Ruth Frankenberg 1997

[69]George.M. Fredrick. Racism a Short History, Princeton University Press. 2002

[70]Eduardo Bonilla-Silva 2006. Race without Racists, Colour blind Racism and the Persistence of Racial Inequality in the United States. Rowman and Littlefield Publishers. 2006.

[71] Karen s. Glover. Racial profiling research, racism and resistance. Rowman and Littlefield Publishers. Pg. 8, 2009

[72]Ibid

[73]Eduardo Bonilla-Silva 2006. Race without Colour-blind Racism and the Persistence of Racial Inequality in the United States. Rowman and Littlefield Publishers. Pg. 37, 2006.Probably no need for full title again just author and page ref

[74]Juan Comas, Racial Myths. The Race Question in Modern Science. Pg. 14. 1992

[75]Ibid

[76] Juan Comas. Race and Science; Racial Myths. Pg. 26-33. New York Columbia,1961

[77]Juan Comas. Race and Science; Racial Myths. Pg.30-31. New York Columbia,1961

[78] Kenneth L. Little. Race and Science: Race and Society. Pg. 59. New York , Columbia University Press ,1961

[79]https://www.thelocal.fr/20160923/stop-forcing-immigrants-to-be-french-and-help-it-happen

[80] Nationalism, Peter Alter,1985

[81]Graham Macklin. The trouble on the Far-right, contemporary right-wing strategies and practices in Europe. Pg. 167-168. 2016

[82]https://www.aljazeera.com/news/2018/11/polish-officials-march-nationalists-independence-day-181111093227508.html

[83]Maik Fielitz, Laura Lotte. Trouble on the Far- Right, introductory remarks, pg. 13-14. 2016

[84]https://www.bbc.com/news/world-europe-37274201

[85]https://www.infomigrants.net/en/post/23294/greece-far-right-activists-in-violent-clashes-to-defend-europe-against-migrants

[86]https://www.die-linke-thl.de/nc/fraktion/aktuell/detail/news/menschen-auf-der-flucht-schuetzen-neonazis-an-grenzen-abweisen/

[87]https://www.humanrightsfirst.org/sites/default/files/Jobbik-Party-Fact-Sheet-final.pdf

[88]https://www.sueddeutsche.de/politik/oesterreich-identitaere-bewegung-1.4384856

[89]MaikFielitz, Laura Lotte Laloire, The Trouble on the Far Right: Contemporary Right-Wing Strategies and Practices in Europe. Pg. 13. 2016

[90]Liz Fekete. The Trouble on the Far Right. Contemporary Right Wing Strategies and Practices in Europe.Pg 28. 2016

[91]ibid.pg.30 2016

[92]https://www.nytimes.com/2019/08/10/world/europe/sweden-immigration-nationalism.html

[93]Maik Fielitz, Laura Lotte Laloire. Trouble on the Far Right: Contemporary Right-Wing Strategies and Practices in Europe. 2016 pg.208

[94]Challenges to democracies in East Central Europe, Jan Holzer, Miroslav mares, Routledge 2017

[95]https://www.bbc.com/news/world-europe-36130006

[96]https://www.nytimes.com/2018/03/31/world/europe/denmark-statue-black-woman.html

[97]Ibid. The sculpture was inspired by Mary Thomas, one of the 'three queens'. Thomas, along with other female leaders, instigated a slave-uprising called the *Fireburn in 1878*. Fifty plantations and most of the towns of Frederiksted on the island of St. Croix in the Danish West Indies were burned down, in what has been called the largest labor revolt in Danish colonial history.

[98] **Vanessa Nakate: Climate activist hits out at 'racist' photo crop**

https://www.bbc.com/news/world-africa-51242972.

[99]Vanessa Nakate: Climate activist hits out at 'racist' photo crop.

https://www.bbc.com/news/world-africa-51242972

[100] Ibid.

[101]White sociologist Dr Robin DiAngelo is addressing a packed auditorium at the University of Sydney's Australian Business School in December 2018. https://www.afr.com/life-and-luxury/arts-and-culture/white-fragility-are-white-people-inherently-racist-20190102-h19mh9

[102]https://en.wikipedia.org/wiki/Expatriate

[103]   https://euro-babble.eu/2019/08/08/espatriati-migranti-rifugiati-perche-dobbiamo-scegliere-le-parole-con-attenzione/

[104]   https://linguisticpulse.com/2015/03/15/expats-and-immigrants-how-we-talk-about-human-migration/

[105]   https://linguisticpulse.com/2015/03/15/expats-and-immigrants-how-we-talk-about-human-migration/

[106]   https://euro-babble.eu/2019/08/08/espatriati-migranti-rifugiati-perche-dobbiamo-scegliere-le-parole-con-attenzione/

[107]   https://ec.europa.eu/eurostat/web/products-eurostat-news/-/DDN-20190315-1?inheritRedirect=true

[108]https://www.theguardian.com/global-development/2019/oct/17/did-a-white-saviours-evangelical-zeal-turn-deadly-uganda-renee-bach-serving-his-children

[109]https://atlantablackstar.com/2019/06/27/renee-bach-a-missionary-playing-doctor-for-years-in-uganda-sued-for-causing-deaths-of-at-least-two-babies/

[110]https://abcnews.go.com/International/renee-bach-doctor-treated-patients-uganda-lawsuit/story?id=63930370

[111]https://www.newyorker.com/magazine/2020/04/13/a-missionary-on-trial

[112] ibid

[113]https://www.newyorker.com/magazine/2020/04/13/a-missionary-on-trial

[114]Teju Cole, 'Known and Strange Things: Essays', Faber & Faber, 2016.

[115]https://www.pri.org/stories/2019-02-08/how-blackface-america-s-first-cultural-export-reinforces-oppression-across-world

[116]https://www.ohchr.org/EN/NewsEvents/Pages/DisplayNews.aspx?NewsID=24153

[117]https://www.theguardian.com/world/2019/sep/18/netherlands-ban-blackface-makeup-zwarte-piet-black-pete-christmas-parade

[118]https://undocs.org/pdf?symbol=ar/A/HRC/39/69/Add.2

[119]https://www.dw.com/en/germanys-anglicism-of-the-year-blackfacing/a-18216479

[120]https://www.bbc.co.uk/newsround/47218511

[121]https://edition.cnn.com/2016/04/01/football/german-football-irpt/index.html

[122]https://www.pri.org/stories/2019-02-08/how-blackface-america-s-first-cultural-export-reinforces-oppression-across-world

[123] https://www.dailymail.co.uk/news/article-4656648/Blackface-ad-Malaysian-beauty-chain-sparks-outrage.html

[124]https://www.pri.org/stories/2019-02-08/how-blackface-america-s-first-cultural-export-reinforces-oppression-across-world

[125]https://wyborcza.pl/piatekekstra/1,129155,15041710,Eugenika__czyli_jak_wyhodowac_nadczlowieka.html

[126]https://www.theguardian.com/commentisfree/2020/feb/19/eugenics-andrew-sabisky-right-ideas-human-breeding

[127]https://wyborcza.pl/piatekekstra/1,129155,15041710,Eugenika__czyli_jak_wyhodowac_nadczlowieka.html

[128] Marius Turda. The History of East-Central European Eugenics, 1900-1945. Bloomsbury Academic, 2017

[129]Marius Turda. The History of East-Central European Eugenics, 1900-1945. Bloomsbury Academic, 2017

[130]Ibid

[131]Ibid

[132]Ibid

[133]https://www.salon24.pl/u/arturbazak/22499,eugenika-koszmar-ktorego-dzisiaj-nikt-nie-pamieta?print=1

[134] Magdalena Garwin. Race and Modernity: History of the Polish Eugenics Movement. Instytut Historii PAN, Wydawnictwo Neriton, pg.25 2003

[135]Ibidpg 26

[136]Ibid pg.27

[137] Ibid pg.27

[138]Ibid

[139] Ibid pg.30-31

[140]https://wiadomosci.gazeta.pl/wiadomosci/7,114883,24266810,o-rydzyk-odradza-sluchaczom-zawierania-malzenstw-mieszanych-to.html?fbclid=IwAR1G2NiwBUVtIl08WfBgv2leZinRXhUjS4uUxEEnHhsO꙰
3

[141]https://wyborcza.pl/piatekekstra/1,129155,15041710,Eugenika__czyli_jak_wyhodowac_nadczlowieka.html

[142]Ibid

[143]Ibid

---

3. https://wiadomosci.gazeta.pl/wiadomosci/7,114883,24266810,o-rydzyk-odradza-sluchaczom-

zawierania-malzenstw-mieszanych-

to.html?fbclid=IwAR1G2NiwBUVtIl08WfBgv2leZinRXhUjS4uUxEEnHhsOWLMPNk6X6fQAq

ew#a_43ec3e5dee6e706af7766fffea512721_167_6cff047854f19ac2aa52aac51bf3af4a_c_43ec3e5dee

6e706af7766fffea512721_154_6cff047854f19ac2aa52aac51bf3af4a_s_43ec3e5dee6e706af7766fffea

512721_BoxNewsMT

[144] Should books with racist content be revised?.https://www.dw.com/en/should-books-with-racist-content-be-revised/g-43308097

[145] Ibid